A m Fields
Rose-Garth
Chapel St
Epworth

SEVEN DAYS OF THE WEEK

Rita F. Snowden

FROM SUNDAY TO MONDAY
A Gateway in Worcester Cathedral

Seven Days of the Week

—oOo—

RITA F. SNOWDEN

Ordinary people, if they want religion at all,
want it to live by, and not merely to think about.

DR W. R. MALTBY

LONDON
THE EPWORTH PRESS

THE EPWORTH PRESS
(FRANK H. CUMBERS)
25-35 City Road, London, E.C.1

MELBOURNE   CAPE TOWN
NEW YORK   TORONTO

SET IN MONOTYPE BEMBO AND PRINTED IN
GREAT BRITAIN BY THE CAMELOT PRESS LTD
LONDON AND SOUTHAMPTON

For my friend

DR F. W. BOREHAM

A little towards a large debt

Contents

INTRODUCTION	xi
STARS ALSO . . .	1
TO ENJOY LIFE	5
MY GOSPEL	8
A SCHOOLBOY'S PRAYER	11
RACHELET'S DILEMMA	14
HANDS AND FEET	17
PRIORITIES	20
MILLIONS OF MIRACLES	24
A POCKETFUL OF MARBLES	28
SUNSET AND SUNRISE	32
A LAMP BURNING BRIGHTLY	35
A SEEKER	38
A WORD FROM RUSSIA	41
NOW	44
GROWING UP	47
FOR DEAR LIFE	51
IS PRAYER FOR BREAD A FARCE?	54
THE MAGIC ATOM	57
TWO WORDS	61
TO SEE THE END	64
LUGGAGE	67
THE FACE ALL-GLORIOUS	70

CLOSE TO LIFE   73

THROUGH THE EYES OF A CHILD   76

STRANGERS NO LONGER   81

A FAVOURITE CHAPTER   84

RINGING WORDS   87

HAPPY PILGRIMS   92

THE LIVING VINE   95

SURE HANDS   99

ONE FAMILY   102

A BIRTHDAY   105

THE HIGH WAYS OF HUMILITY   108

CROWDS   110

WELL MET   114

HANDS   117

AFTER EASTER   120

AN INTRODUCER   124

WORDS AND DEEDS   127

List of Illustrations

FROM SUNDAY TO MONDAY   *frontispiece*

GOD'S GIFT OF HARVEST   *facing page* 10

A MIRACLE   ,,   ,,   58

PRINCE AND DARLING—FAITHFUL WORKERS   ,,   ,,   106

ix

Introduction

WHICH is your favourite day of the week? Each day seems to have a colour and character all its own. Monday seems the least liked of all the days. Is it because it stands on the frontier between worship and work, between the sacred and the secular? The feeling about Monday is so general that the colloquialism 'Mondayish' has had to be admitted to the dictionary. If you feel differently about it, it may be that you are a cobbler or a parson.

In olden times, Monday was humorously canonized 'St Monday', the feast of cobblers, because they could never remember which was the feast day of their patron-saint—save that it was a Monday. So they celebrated it every Monday. But I am afraid that happy state of affairs has been a little tightened up. As long ago as when Swift was writing his famous letters to Stella, he wrote: 'Monday is parson's holiday.' But even in the Church that is not now as it used to be. That it is well-earned and needed can be recognized without remembering that the most depressed entries in the diary of Robertson of Brighton— the great preacher of last century—were always on a Monday. Today the demands of an effective ministry are much more exacting. And it is much more difficult to observe 'parson's holiday'.

According to the dictionary, 'Mondayish' is the sense of 'feeling slack after the week-end'. It is the mood that the rhymster yawningly sets down in his heavy-footed verse:

> Yonder see the morning blink,
> The sun is up, and up must I
> To wash and dress and eat and drink,
> And look at things and talk and think
> And work, and God knows why.

Now you do not need to remind me that the person who writes like that has not been to worship on Sunday. He has much more likely been to the beach, or he has been golfing, or tinkering with his car. On Monday he knows what feeling 'Mondayish' is—and so do his home-folk. For such, Monday is not a good day; it is a day of severe testing.

But for those of us who go to worship on Sunday—and so make much better use of the first day of the week—Monday is still a day of testing. Hugh Redwood, the well-known modern newspaperman, writing his autobiography *Bristol Fashion*, tells of his conversion. 'The first day of my new life,' says he, 'was a Monday, but the feeling with which I awoke to it was the reverse of that with which Monday mornings are proverbially associated. . . . Instead of a fading vision I grasped a clear-cut reality.'

'A fading vision' or a 'clear-cut reality'. That is well put. From the very start, Hugh Redwood's religion thus proclaimed itself real and vital. How do I know that? There was no observable break between Sunday and Monday—between worship and work, between things sacred and secular.

And that was what attracted Anne Treneer to Will Richards, in the little place where she grew up, in Cornwall. He was the blacksmith, and every Monday morning he was at his work beside his stone-built forge—his sleeves rolled, his strong arms brown and muscular, the neck-band of his shirt unbuttoned, his cap on his head. The great cart-horses might be seen standing in his little yard, waiting their turn. Will might be heard, as well as seen, masterfully dealing with one of them: 'Woa-up! Woa-back!' But there was much more to Will than that. 'Will was genial in dealing with people,' says Miss Treneer, 'but not so tactful as to be tame or smooth. His feelings showed, and he could be hot-hearted; but there was something in him immensely reassuring and kind. He was at once human and God-fearing without a trace of cant. Children felt safe and not silly with Will. "Hullo! my dear," he would say, "Hullo!" We were reassured and knew we were welcome. He used to whistle hymn-tunes; not a few confined favourites, but dozens of different tunes. With them he carried his Sundays into his week-days. Let me say that again: 'with them'—his whistling of hymn tunes—'he carried his Sundays into his week-days'. And isn't that something we've all got to do; not perhaps like Will, in whistling hymns, or in singing them, if that suits us better, but in our attitude to life, and particularly to work? If our religion is to be at all relevant to the strains and stresses of this day in which we live, it must survive the test of Monday.

It is good that we should meet for worship on Sunday—we can scarcely over-emphasize the value of it in these days of rush and tear, and nervous tension—but there is much more to it than that. There is the challenge that meets us on Monday morning. How does religion look then? What does it do for us then? And through us, what does it do for the world of which we are a part? For religion, if it is to be vital, is not something that makes some difference to a few things, but something that makes all the difference to everything. God is not left behind in Church, on the far side of Monday; God is present in every moment of all our days, and is involved in every choice that we make, in every penny that we earn, and spend, in every attitude that we adopt, in every task that we take up.

Hugh Redwood crossed over from Sunday to Monday, and so too did Will Richards, without any visible break. But city or country, time or place, have really nothing to do with it. The question is whether our religion is real or not. Lord Moynihan, the distinguished surgeon of our own day, like these others, found himself often called upon to operate in the presence of other surgeons. At the conclusion of one such operation, a young doctor said to him, with understandable pride and respect: 'It must be very difficult for you to operate with a group of us watching your every move.' 'Well,' said Lord Moynihan, 'it is like this: there are just three people in the theatre when I operate—the patient and myself.'

'Three?' said the young man, 'but that is only two—who is the third?'

The distinguished surgeon answered quietly: 'God.'

I repeat: religion is not something that makes some difference to a few things, but something that makes all the difference to everything.

Stars Also . . .

TONIGHT, as I walked home to our peaceful hilltop, a 'plane went overhead. It was too velvety dark to see more than the tiny lights on its wing-tips.

I have flown a great deal over the familiar farmlands and forests of my own little country; over its sunlit beaches and silver-wraithed mountain-tops. I have flown over the vast spaces of our neighbouring continent, up along Australia's surf-fringed coast, into her tropical jungle-lands of the north; over palm-fringed islands beautiful in themselves, and set in cobalt seas; into the mighty Inland, over desert and rocks of a fiery cinnabar the land veined with the mauve and blue of arid river-beds.

A very different picture spread beneath me as I flew over the green, intimate beauty of England; over Scotland; over Ireland with its Lilliputian, patchwork fields. In Switzerland, too, there were tiny fields in hay-time; mountains as well, menacing and majestic.

I shall never forget my experiences of flying during the hours of night; of coming in over great cities—London with its myriad lights, Amsterdam with its girdle of silver water-ways, and San Francisco with its mighty spread—above all, of flying under the stars over great oceans when most if not all of one's companions were asleep. Mystery was in that experience, and God.

Sir Miles Thomas, formerly Chairman of the British Overseas Airways Corporation, feels much the same about night flying. A religious man, brought up among the warm-hearted people of Wales, he came early under the influence of their religion. In boyhood he was enthralled, but as his questioning mind hardened, doubts crept in. 'Then,' he said, 'came my initiation

I

to airmanship. . . . On the stick-and-string aeroplanes of those days, with their slow speed and short range, navigation was not very difficult, and we youngsters were taught about the celestial bodies. Gazing into the heavens one quiet, star-studded night I suddenly realized that although I could readily understand that a star might be so many millions of miles away, that even its light took years to reach me, I could not hope to comprehend the infinity of the dark blue spaces in between the stars. I realized then that the human mind is finite. There are certain things that we simply cannot grasp, and in that humility I rediscovered my full faith in the old religion.'

The little world that we each know is at some time or other filled with mystery; we have each our 'dark blue spaces in between the stars'. The experience has nothing to do with flying, only with the strange business of living.

Sometimes we find ourselves thrust into this area of mystery with dramatic suddenness; there is an accident, a cry. Or there is a grave illness, a doctor's verdict; and how dark is the night! Or there is that creeping, insidious thing, infidelity, and we can see no plain way into the future! Then our human spirits look up for those things that alter not, those sure points of light beyond earth's giving; we must have our stars.

You and I do not speak much about these experiences, though we know them; we each have our 'dark blue spaces in between the stars'.

But thank God, we have our stars, too. How could we continue in this strange business of living, if it were not so?

What Bishop Hanns Lilje did in the hour of his testing is but a parable. Arrested in Hanover in 1944, he was imprisoned in the upper story of a forbidding place in Berlin. And night after night air-raids were centred on the city. Then that sensitive soul had to sit alone in his little cell, at the mercy, it seemed, of cruel tyrants. There he knew, if any man in modern times ever did, 'the dark blue spaces in between the stars'. Yet when the air-raid warnings sounded, and his guards scuttled below for what safety they could find, in that moment of eternity when the searchlights silently picked out the menace before the anti-aircraft guns went into action, that Christian man did one thing.

He moved to the darkened window of his tiny cell, and knocked down the black-out curtains so that he might look up at the stars!

The natural darkness above his head was not one whit darker than the darkness that was about his spirit; but there were stars there, too.

While I was in New York, at Riverside Church, I learned of a young Negro minister who came suddenly into 'the dark blue spaces in between the stars'. His young wife died. But whilst the night was still about him, he chanced to hear a sympathetic voice on the wireless. It was the voice of that good and wise preacher, Dr Harry Fosdick. And as the young Negro listened he found himself saying: 'There is a man who will understand and help me.' And with that he set out for the vast, impersonal, city of New York, to the church where Dr Fosdick had been sent of God to minister.

At the close of a long consultation, when he who had been hurt and mystified came out of the room, he was heard to say, half to himself, half to the young girl who gave him his hat: 'What a man! When I went in there all the stars had dropped out. . . . But one by one he has put them all in again!'

He was right—gloriously right! But he was wrong—gloriously wrong! The stars had never dropped out! Like so many of us, he had become so taken up with the mystery of 'the dark blue spaces' that he'd forgotten the stars.

The stars are always steady! Jesus found it so in the very darkest night of experience. Three great facts were His stars, fashioned of the unchanging character of God; His power, His love, His nearness. And those three stars shine steady in our night; no man can put them there, or take them away.

That is not to say that we have done with mystery, with hurt, sorrow, suffering, or whatever it is that makes up for us 'the dark blue spaces in between the stars'. Jesus hung upon the Cross, and suffered the greatest darkness, the greatest mystery that this world can know, so that He cried out: 'My God, why . . . ?' But in a moment—if I may say it reverently—He had pushed away the black-out curtains, and those three stars were shining still, so that He cried: 'Father, into Thy hands I commend my spirit!'

And that is the highest and best we can do, and it is enough: to cast ourselves upon the unchanging character of God, upon His power, His love, His nearness.

To Enjoy Life

EVERY time I think of Temple Gairdner, it is as if a shaft of sunlight comes into my days. That was a power he had that made him most like his Lord. Life for him was wide and deep, and full of rich joy. Men loved to seek him out in his rooms in Oxford; there was something so vital in his friendship. It was good to remember how he talked and how he looked; to carry in the mind's eye a picture of him walking up and down the ancient ways of thought and experience, rejoicing in the common gifts of God, calling upon the delphiniums and the azaleas in the garden bed to praise Him, standing silent in the dawn, or kneeling humbly before the mystery of love in the college chapel. And when his days in Oxford were exchanged for strenuous days of missionary leadership in Cairo, the story was the same. Great sorrows fell upon him there, but he ended his service with praise and joy. It was said of those who went to see him when he was ill, that they couldn't bear to leave: his room was full of kindness. Not even death could quench his love of life—and enjoyment of it. Said one of his close friends: 'One couldn't give a list of the things he enjoyed. Beauty of sound, beauty of shape, of colour, of movement, beauty of scent. He enjoyed the pleasure of creative work, of the reception of the great work of other minds; he enjoyed children's parties, and mangoes, Charlie Chaplin, treacle tarts, swimming, bores, kedgeree, analysing sensations, geology, charades!'

An odd list! But no more odd than a telling over of the things his Master enjoyed must have seemed to those who knew Him in His daily life in Palestine.

Many were moved to question the religious credentials of Jesus when they saw the kind of things He enjoyed. His eye seemed to miss none of the ordinary affairs that went on about

5

Him, and His heart refused nothing that was human. Sunlight and shadow were alike gifts of God, to be richly enjoyed; the sower trudging up and down his sweet-smelling furrow, the wild flower by the way, the merchant, the tenant, the father and son, the little child at his play. Religious leaders before Him might ponder, or teach in places specially set apart for their purpose; not so Jesus. He refused from the start their little tidy dividing-lines between sacred and secular. He could fast in the wilderness, but He could enjoy a wedding-feast so whole-heartedly that His very presence turned 'water into wine', in more senses than one. Again and again, He was guest at a party —with Simon, with Zacchæus—until His welcome confounded His critics. 'John the Baptist came neither eating nor drinking,' they said, 'and this Man comes both eating and drinking. And what is more'—the tone of their accusation seemed to underline —'*He enjoys it!*'

It was no accident; it was the outward manifestation of His inmost nature. In the face of their accusing, He likened Himself and His little group of disciples to a 'bridal party'. Jewish Law exempted a bridal party from fasting—others fasted twice in the week, Mondays and Thursdays—but Jesus said, with a smile playing about His eyes: 'We are as a bridal-party: do the friends of the bridegroom fast while he is with them?'

He enjoyed the good, simple, normal things of life, such as hospitality of heart, and home; He was more than once in Peter's home, near the boats and nets, and He was often in the home of Mary and Martha and Lazarus at Bethany. He begged a cool drink from a woman He met at a well—a thing that no religious leader had ever done before, so that it shocked His friends. He spread a picnic meal for five thousand hungry people out for the day; He enjoyed sound sleep with His head on a fisherman's pillow in the end of a boat; He ended with a last supper the ministry He had begun at a wedding-feast, and on His lips many and many a time between, were the words: 'Be of good cheer!'

He enjoyed life; enjoyed it deeply as the good gift of God. It was an enjoyment that went deeper than a good strong body, interesting and stimulating friends, and fortuitous events—far

6

deeper. It was never for one moment at the mercy of things that could happen; it was rooted in the nature of God the Father, the great Giver of all good things to be enjoyed.

And that was the secret that Paul had in mind when he wrote to his young and beloved Timothy: 'Charge them that are rich in this world, that they be not high-minded, nor trust in uncertain riches, but in the living God who giveth us richly all things to enjoy' (1 Timothy 6[17]).

The heart of the secret lies in the wondrous fact that God first giveth us Himself. Today, our religion misses something of eternal significance in our neglect to ask the age-old question: 'What is the chief end of man?' and to respond gladly with the answer: 'To glorify God and to enjoy Him for ever.' That, simply put, was the secret of Jesus.

After talking with Walter de la Mare, Siegfried Sassoon said he went away 'for a while seeking the world with re-christened eyes'. And that's how people felt who knew Jesus. There was something so vital about Him, that life was never the same again; their enjoyment of God, and life's experience, was something so much more than a Sunday smattering of dull grey generalities.

My Gospel

DO you know 'the gospel according to Samuel'? I confess I had not heard of it, until lately when I talked with an old preacher grown grey in the service of truth. But his eyes were full of light when I questioned him about the four Gospels—Matthew, Mark, Luke and John. I was curious to know which of them had brought him into the Kingdom, and not ready for the surprise in store for me.

'My dear,' he began, taking his time, 'I owe an incalculable debt to each—to Matthew, who wrote for the Jews, to Mark, to Luke, to John. But I didn't get to know them till I was in my twenties; and I came into the Kingdom when I was nineteen. It was "the gospel according to Samuel" that did it.'

Noting my puzzled look, he went on: 'Old Sam Allen was a farmer in the little place where I grew up; and a better man I've never met to this hour. He was good to his family, and loyal to his church, and he could plough a straighter furrow than anybody I ever knew. He wasn't much with words—but,' he added, 'there was something about his life day by day that no lad could miss. So—in answer to your question—I came into the Kingdom with all my young eagerness, won by "the gospel according to Samuel"!'

And more and more, as I have pondered it, I have found a wonder in that surprise answer. For it is still true, that

> *The dear Lord's best interpreters*
> *Are humble human souls;*
> *The gospel of a life like theirs*
> *Is more than books or scrolls.*

That's what John McNeill, the Scottish evangelist had in

mind when he said: 'The gospel I preach is "the gospel according to John".'

And there was nothing unsound or novel about that, though he was blessed with a better gift of words than the old farmer, Samuel Allen. The Rev. John McNeill knew, that it was not only in the words that were given him to utter, but rather in what he was in himself, that his gospel consisted. Preaching was, he knew—in essence—'the communication of truth, through personality'.

Twice Paul set down those surprising words: 'According to my gospel' (once in Romans 2^{16}; and again in 2 Timothy 2^8). At first, his words sound presumptuous: '*My* gospel—*my* gospel'. But surely it was Christ's gospel! Yes. The Gospel, the good Anglo-Saxon translation of the Greek 'evangel', was the good tidings, the good news, that Christ brought to the world, that could come through no one else. So it was Christ's gospel. In that sense the word was used to express the story of Christ.

Then it came to be used for the book in which the story was related—in the sense in which we speak of the four Gospels of the New Testament.

But Paul uses it in a still wider sense, as it is used elsewhere in the New Testament, for the essential, living message of which the four Gospels are the story.

And when Paul uses it in this sense, he is not content to talk about '*the*' gospel, it is '*my*' gospel. It is not a matter of pure intellect, or something at second-hand; it is at the very centre of his being; so that now when he shares it, it is not the gospel according to Matthew, Mark, Luke and John, or Barnabas or James, or anyone else. It is Jesus Christ, 'according to my gospel'. It is his own soul's apprehension of his Saviour.

That, of course, is the only gospel that anyone of us has to share. As someone has said, 'the Gospels are not four, but ten thousand times ten thousand and thousands and thousands'. That does not mean that the glorious truth that Christ came to bring is distorted to a thousand meanings—far from it. It means rather that the wondrous truth cannot be *fully* represented by any one of us. So rich and full is the gospel of Christ, that

9

when each of us has witnessed to the utmost of his ability, there is still much to tell. But each of us can best bring glory to Christ, by being faithful, *according to his own gospel*.

For the truth—and it's a very challenging truth—is that this is the only way the Gospel will ever come to some. Some are careless about turning the pages of the sacred Book; some do not readily understand what they read there; but they are arrested, and enriched by what comes to them in dependable, warm-hearted, living form. Many years ago, Oxford was visited by an outbreak of dread sickness. Anxiety and death entered many homes, and the Vicar of St Mary's, along with others, found himself hard-pressed to bring the gospel of Christ to needy hearts. In one of the back streets he visited a woman, who, as she lay dying, cried out against the Church and the ministry of religion. The good Vicar, called to her bedside, strove in vain to win from her any faint affirmation of faith. He took out his New Testament, and read to her some of the greatest passages in the Gospels. She appeared to be unable to grasp what the words were meant to convey. But there was with him a Sister of the Incarnation, a very friend of sinners, known and loved in all the mean, back streets. The Vicar, bringing her forward, asked: 'If you do not believe in God, do you believe in Sister Marion?' Ah, that was different. It was no appeal through words in a book, or through an article of the Church's faith couched in theological terms, but through a living, warm-hearted Christian soul whom she knew. And looking up into the Sister's face, she smiled and murmured: 'I believe in God. . . . Jesu, have mercy', and fell alseep.

That but serves to underline the challenge. Not even Paul's gospel is enough for me: the best I have to offer is 'Christ, according to *my* gospel', my Lord, and my God.

GOD'S GIFT OF HARVEST

A Schoolboy's Prayer

I DO not wonder that my friend, Adrian's mother, was a little taken-aback when she discovered that Adrian had changed his form of prayer. As a little fellow Adrian had been taught to use the words of a prayer of his mother's choosing. And then the time had come for him to leave that behind and frame the wording of his own prayer, and say it alone. It was at this point of change that his mother felt uneasy, for out of the blue he announced one night: 'When I was small I used to pray, "God bless Mummy, Daddy and Martin, and make me a good boy". But I don't say that now.'

'Oh, don't you?' answered his mother. 'What do you say?'

And then came Adrian's honest boy's answer: 'I just say, "God bless the lot of us"!'

I do not wonder at his mother's concern, for what Adrian had done was far-reaching. Instead of Mummy, Daddy, Martin and himself named before God as individuals, they were now being lumped together, and something essential lost.

If not in our school years, some of us in our twenties, thirties, forties, fifties, find ourselves adopting the same attitude. And it has far-reaching results. Dr Fosdick is right: 'One of the root reasons why prayer becomes merely a pious form is that, while people believe in God in a general and vague fashion, they do not vividly grasp the idea that God cares for, and is dealing with, every one of us!' Some of us find that a difficult thing to believe. The universe is so immense. On some star-filled night, we find ourselves out of doors, and we look up, and we are awed at what we see. The stars are so many, and so great, that we find ourselves mere nothings beneath the creative greatness of God. We can at least feel for our contemporary poet, V. Sackville-West, when she says: 'My religion, if I have one, can be resolved into the few words, "I simply do not know". Who am I to pretend to know? I am less than a speck of dust on a speck of a satellite revolving around a speck of a star, which we on earth are pleased to call the Sun, but which in fact is only an insignificant member of one galaxy in a universe which we know to contain a million other galaxies of equal size, whose origin is obscure to us, but whose date is supposed by present-day scientists to go back four-thousand-million years.'

It is useless to argue that the universe is as it has ever been; it is not. Our universe is infinitely greater—or at least our conception of it is—than that, for instance, which the Psalmist knew, when he stood out under the few stars visible to his naked eye, and cried with awe: 'What is man that thou art mindful of him?' Only a lifetime ago Lord Kelvin caused a stir by calculating the number of the stars as a thousand million. Today, our astronomers tell us quite calmly that the host above our heads might more truly be estimated as many times that number.

As well as the size of the universe, there is its age. When we were little Adrian's size, we looked with awe at a date in the margin of our Bibles—in the book of Genesis—and read as the birthday of the world, 4004 B.C. But today we know that Archbishop Ussher, who worked out that date, was far out in his reckoning. The story of God's creation, as it appears in that book, remains, but not the date; it was a puny human mind that penned that into the margin.

Nor can we escape consideration of the power of the world, in which for a little time we must make our home. If that power, in one atom bomb, can completely wipe out in a moment of time a place the size of Hiroshima, what is the value of the individual? How can you matter? How can I matter in such a world?

As well as the size and age and power of the universe, there is also the work that many of us have to do. There was a time when the boss knew each worker, and morning by morning, greeted each by name, ' 'Lo, Jim!' ' 'Lo, Jean!' But that time has quite gone for many—Jim and Jean are swallowed up in what has been called 'the gross impersonality of modern industry'. They are referred to today as 'personnel'. *The Times* was right: 'It is doubtful whether a more degrading, a more ill-favoured synonym for two or more members of the human race has ever been coined. People to whom it applies do not "have", they are "in possession of"; they cannot "eat", they "consume"; instead of "homes", they have "places of residence", in which, instead of "living", they are "domiciled". In short, they are not people at all, they are personnel.'

How can you and I pray, or live, when we cease to think of ourselves as individuals, and only know ourselves, in this awe-inspiring world, lumped together in general existence, under the term, 'God bless the lot of us'?

The plain, simple truth—as plain and simple as Christianity—is that in such conditions we cannot live. And God means us to know it. The supreme revelation of Himself to us, is that above all He is our Father. And what an amazing piece of truth that is! For *the essential of true fatherhood is individual care for the child.* 'Love,' as one has put it, 'has an individualizing power.' The size or age of the family dwelling—the house of the earthly family, or the world of God's family—has nothing to do with it. Nor has the size of the child—baby or grown son—or the size of the family. 'Say not I shall never be missed in a boundless creation' (Ecclesiasticus 16[17]). Again and again, in His stories—of the one coin, of the one sheep, and, most unforgettably, of the son lost in the far country and restored—Jesus shows us how God the loving Father deals with each individual child, and values each individual child. That, to me, is one of the most important pieces of truth in existence. It makes it possible for me to live in this kind of world, and to do the work that I must. I can never get lost. Everything is different now, because God is my Father.

Rachelet's Dilemma

I WOULD like to ask you a question, but I have no right to ask it. How often do you pray? Don't tell me that you don't pray. I have never met a person who doesn't pray—when in a fix, if at no other time.

J. M. Scott has lately shown us old Rachelet, the vine-grower, in his little French valley. 'The flowering went well. The early summer was cool and rather damp. Then the dry heat came. . . . The latter half of July was almost intolerably hot. There was no cloud in the sky and no breath of wind. The air was stale and heavy. . . . Each morning when he left his cottage Rachelet looked anxiously at the sky. He well knew that the only way such weather could break was in a thunderstorm. And thunder often brought hail. So late in the season, hail would not only destroy the present crop but that of the next year also, for if the shoots were broken off there would be no bearers next spring for the new shoots to sprout from.

On 20th July there came news that several vineyards in Alsace had been battered to pieces by hailstones. (The same thing happened at much the same date in 1952.) Alsace—that was far enough away. But next day Rachelet heard on the radio of thunderstorms with hail in the Loire valley. They were said to be moving southwards. He wondered by what route they could come. It was far from certain that the bad weather would pass over Mèdoc. But it might.

'When darkness fell, the sky to the north glowed now and then with lightning. Rachelet estimated that the storm must be over Angou-lême. He telephoned to a friend who lived there.

'What he was told was not encouraging. Hail-stones as large as sparrows' eggs had broken a number of windows before the storm passed.

' "In what direction was it travelling?" Rachelet asked.
' "In your direction."

'Rachelet hung up the receiver, picturing the vineyard bare as in midwinter except that the ground would be strewn with grapes and leaves. What made it still worse was that the *patron* was away on holiday and he would have to tell him about it when he returned.

'There was nothing to be done except wait. . . . The lightning was growing brighter and the thunder more loud. There was no longer any reasonable chance that the storm would miss them. Rachelet wanted to pray, but he was ashamed to. He had never been much of a one for the forms of religion, and to call upon God only when he was in trouble seemed dishonest. At last he put it like this: "Lord, I am in your hands. It is your storm, but I am responsible for this vineyard. I only mention that the sea is very close and hail would do no damage there." ' Bless him!

Have we not all found ourselves in a like fix? The prayer that rises instinctively to our lips—despite all our arguments against it—is what I call an emergency prayer. It is the prayer of the Psalmist: 'Hear me speedily, O Lord.'

We don't know what particular emergency gave rise to that prayer of the Psalmist; but we know our own experience. 'He that would learn to pray,' said George Herbert, 'Let him go to sea.' He might as well have said, 'Let him tend a vineyard when thunderstorms threaten', or 'Let him be responsible for a tiny child through teething, mumps or pneumonia', or 'Let him tear open an urgent telegram bearing grim news of one very dear to him', or 'Let him be involved in an accident'.

Dear old Rachelet we know—he is one with us; and his prayer is instinct with the same urgency as our own prayers. Some of us have felt just as shy about offering prayers at all. But the fact is we can't help it. As one grasps at some fixed object when falling, so we intuitively reach out after something or someone more than our own strength, and we pray with the Psalmist: 'Hear me speedily, O Lord!'

But the emergency prayer—for all that it is as natural as anything we do, and as desperately earnest—I am bound to

15

admit, brings us scarcely half-way into the true experience of prayer, and the Psalmist was not slow to know it. Following on his human cry that we all understand: 'Hear me speedily, O Lord', is this complementary cry, 'Cause me to hear . . . for I lift up my soul unto thee'; and the two are set down in successive verses in Psalm 143 for our guidance. The first, of course, is *petition*—full of clamour, claiming a hearing. The second is *communion*—full of quiet, giving a hearing.

Our little emergency prayers in no wise exhaust the possibilities of prayer. Our cries, natural as they are, spontaneous, shy at times, reach up to God, full of desperation; but His words to us come down fraught with peace, and quiet strength, and eternal love. So that the experience of communion is always more than the experience of petition, because God, the loving Father of our spirits, with whom we can have day to day communion, is Himself far more than any gift He can give us, even though it may be some earnestly-sought deliverance in a moment of emergency.

I would like to ask you a question, but I have no right to. How often do you pray—like that?

Hands and Feet

A LITTLE higher up the hill from where we live at 'West Hills', is a home for deaf and dumb children. Quite often on Saturdays we see them coming down the hill for a walk. They form at one and the same time a pathetic and a hopeful little company. A great deal is being done for them, and they seem very happy. Their odd, guttural efforts at speech are very inadequate, but they have other ways of communicating their ideas; they learn to lip-read, and they speak with their hands.

When I was their age, the possibility of speaking with one's hands appealed to me as great fun, and I studied it whenever I had a moment to spare, watching the cows as they grazed on the roadside, or sitting before the fire at night. In a treasured, dog-eared copy of *The Girls Own Paper* that came my way, was a page of drawings of hands, showing how it might be done—the alphabet from A to Z. I tried it on my friends at school, but it was never more serious than a game, since I was blessed with a good tongue and ears, and had no need to speak with my hands.

As the children passed today, I fell to wondering if their method was the same, but they were too quick for me. In any case, I found I had forgotten most of what I had learned.

I recalled instead, a strange text out of Proverbs. It concerns a 'worthless person', but it says of him: 'He speaketh with his feet.' So as I went on with my task in the garden, I passed in my thought from speaking with one's hands to speaking with one's feet.

I am not sure how the worthless person of Proverbs spoke with his feet, but I know how a good many worthwhile people do it. Booth-Tucker, the saint who served in the ranks of the Salvation Army in India, came to my mind. He loved the people, but his efforts to share the story of his Lord with them by word of mouth met only with indifference, even opposition.

Then a day came that changed everything. He had been cruelly treated, and, driven from a village where he had received even less welcome than usual, ill and alone, he lay down beneath a tree and fell into unconsciousness.

When he wakened, he found to his astonishment the same group of village-people who had thrust him out of their village, shedding tears upon his feet. When he sought the reason for their changed behaviour, their reply was one that he never forgot. They had followed him from the village, meaning to do him further hurt, but when they came across him lying unconscious they had seen his feet. And they had noticed for the first time that he walked barefoot on the roads, even as they did, and when they saw his feet, unaccustomed to shoe-less travel, stone-wounded and bleeding, their hearts were melted toward him. *He had spoken to them with his feet.* And with a rising sense of shame for their treatment of him, they carried him back into their village, and ministered to him. Now they were ready to listen to the message of him whose words they had so long, and so strenuously resisted.

And many another who has passed this way has done the same thing, though not perhaps in the same setting. The thousand steps of a mother as she goes about her work in the home are one of the ways in which she tells of her love. She never counts the steps she takes; it is her way of speaking with her feet.

When someone commiserated with Florence Banks, a lady of good works—the kind of good works that mean an opportunity for someone in the community, and a gleam of hope through the darkest day—she did not deny that hers was tiring service. 'It's too bad that you have to be on your feet so much,' said the kindly soul. Miss Banks's reply was surely a classic one: 'I think feet were meant to be on.' She did not need to summon many words; her feet said, day by day, so much to those who cared to notice her coming and going.

And that was true about our Lord. Luke set it down in simple words: 'He went about doing good.' His feet, sandal-shod, often dusty and weary, took Him amongst men and women with

18

common needs. They enabled Him to pause a moment beside a well, as He journeyed, to talk with a woman of Samaria; they took Him with all haste to the side of Mary and Martha in their grief; they led Him at last steadfastly toward Jerusalem, and to the crowning task of His life.

Today, those of us who follow in His way, must also learn to speak with our feet. Kagawa's words are a shock for those of us who think that following Him is a task we can take lightly. Says he:

> I read
> In a book
> That a man called
> CHRIST
> Went about doing good.
>
> It is very disconcerting
> To me
> That I am so easily
> Satisfied
> With just
> Going about.

Priorities

IT hardly matters where we live, we can lift up our eyes and see building going on these days. New houses have a way of springing up like mushrooms, or so it seems to those of us who watch the surrender of the green countryside. But some of us are more intimately involved, with all the patience-exhausting issues of site, size and cost. It must be a little easier to move into a house that someone else has built—the Government, or the firm for which one works—but whichever way it is, a great many choices have still to be made.

For a move is something far more than moving the chairs, and the beds, and the bit of carpet that will have to do until we can manage something better. It's a matter of priorities. They haven't changed since Isaac moved his family, and that was rather a long time ago. The setting, of course, is different—a camel-hair tent then sufficed: there was no wireless and carpet —but the essentials are the same. As H. V. Morton reminds us: 'The only things that change radically in life are fashions and inventions. The human heart was patented long ago, and the Creator has not seen fit to bring out a later model.'

So it is worth discovering how Isaac managed. It is clearly set out in Genesis 26[25]; there is no uncertainty about Isaac's priorities. 'He built an altar there . . . and pitched his tent there . . . and there Isaac's servants digged a well.' Notice the order: first worship—he built an altar; then home—he pitched his tent; and then work—the well.

In that there is a great secret for us, however sophisticated we are, however well-served by the miracle of modern science and the Welfare State. Religion, home, and work are still the great essentials, and it is fatal to divorce them.

Despite the fact that Isaac must have had a good deal to do in moving—as we all have—immediately the new site was reached he set about gathering stones and pieces of rock to raise an altar. And there he and his family worshipped, and sought the blessing of God on their new enterprise.

In raising the altar first, he was doing what men and women of every age and clime have done in some fashion. He was recognizing a capacity for God; he was recognizing that the make-up of himself, and each of his family, was three-fold, and thus grander than the beasts of the fields. And we stand exactly where Isaac and his family stood in this; we have our bodies to nourish, so we make our way to the grocers and the butchers, and we set to work to make something of our gardens, and we spend hours each day between the stove and the sink. We have our minds, so we raise our schools—even though at start they lack playgrounds and footpaths—and as soon as possible, our libraries. But grander still, we have our spirits, and unless we raise our altars—Sunday-schools and churches—that part of our nature that most resembles God must starve.

The altar is an essential, not an addition that can be given attention when everything else is going well—our houses built, our gardens laid out, our shops flourishing. Nothing, Isaac would say to us out of his experience, must precede the worship of God. The law of life is 'righteousness exalteth a nation', and we cannot break that law—we can only break our family life and our national life upon it. We are made that way.

Ill success attends those who, moving on to new ground, fail to raise the altar. There was a stage when it was thought best to civilize the Maori people, and then Christianize them. So the Church of England Missionary Society sent out to New Zealand shoemakers and blacksmiths and carpenters to prepare the way for the later coming of the Gospel. But it was a mistake. And some while later those in authority realized it, and sent out to those self-same Maori people of human needs and fears and passions, Samuel Marsden, to meet them on Christmas Day, 1814, with the message: 'Behold, I bring you good tidings of great joy', and to raise an altar, and call upon the name of the Lord. We should be foolish, shouldn't we, in moving on to new ground, to make that mistake over again?

Let us raise our altar, let us gather there with our families, even if at first it is only in a modest pre-fab building; let us make sure that we do not slacken our reverence for things sacred. As Nels Ferré says in his little book *Return to Christianity*: 'Let us worship God. In worship we behold the goodness of God, and become partakers of that goodness; in worship we see the patience of God and become partakers of that patience; we celebrate the purpose of God and offer ourselves as servants of that purpose.'

After raising the altar, Isaac pitched his tent; he set up his family home. He was a home-lover, and there is something wrong with anyone who is not. And there is something wrong with any new house—however deep its foundations, wide its views, and satisfactory its drainage and lighting—that is not a home. It is people, close-linked in unselfish relationships, who make homes. Homes are not contractors materials, or even adequate meals and stainless sinks and pay-envelopes. Homes are men and women, little children and young folk, living together in rich partnership, discharging the total responsibilities of the corporate life. Nowhere else can we so early and so easily learn life's real values—to rejoice in our energies, to reverence things sacred, to respect the rights of others. And what is more important in our world today? We must tie together all that is richest at the altar with all that is most rewarding in the home. Isaac has shown us clearly how they stand in relationship to each other.

And then there was the well. The digging of that well was again something essential to life—and really hard work, in that climate. Heated and weary, with primitive tools—there was no well-boring apparatus in those days—they had to dig deeply through the porous lime-stone rock, to where the rain had filtered through to the hard stratum beneath. Even when the well had been dug and the waters released, there yet remained the hard work of keeping the well open, of combating the drifting sand, and safeguarding it from abuse; and there was no escaping at any time the physical labour of hauling up the precious water a vesselful at a time. If the well stood for refreshment and life, there was no doubt that it stood also for hard work.

People talked once as if work was a punishment imposed; but since then we have had the revelation of Jesus: we have seen Him in the carpenter's workshop; we have heard Him say: 'My Father worketh hitherto, and I work.' Now any pity we have is for the man or woman who has no work.

> *Thank God for work!*
> *Once man's penance, now his rich reward.*
> *For work to do, and strength to do the work,*
> *We thank Thee, Lord.*

But Isaac's three-fold secret must stand, if life is to render up to us its richest satisfactions. The rising cost of living may whip us to work like slaves, but if our work is to have any meaning it must be linked with our homes, as of necessity both must be linked to our worship. Worship—home—work! Thank God for these three great priorities!

Millions of Miracles

I SAW a miracle today—saw it with my own eyes, and in our own garden—a perfectly-fashioned red rose. It was rich in fragrance, and the dew was on it. I can only call it a miracle, when I think of the fresh clay of our newly cultivated garden whence those lovely qualities came. You may object that I use the term 'miracle' rather freely. I remember Arnold Bennett's words of the ecstatic young man in love. 'My boy, she is simply miraculous,' he exclaimed. 'But,' retorted Bennett, 'a girl cannot be called a miracle. If a girl is to be called a miracle, then you might call pretty nearly anything a miracle.' And he added, as truly and gladly: 'That is just it: you might. You can. You ought.'

That the red rose happens to be the first to break from our clay, or the girl the first to answer the love of the lad, has nothing to do with it, though we are liable to think it has. It is curious that we should. If once in a century these things should happen, people would flock from the ends of the earth to see them. As the poet says:

> If the good God were suddenly
> To make a solitary Blind to see,
> We would stand wondering all
> And call it miracle;
> But that He gives with lavish hand
> Sight to a million souls, we stand
> And say, with little awe,
> He but fulfils a natural law!

Walt Whitman says: 'To me every hour of the light and dark is a miracle.' I am sure he is right. But isn't it true that most of us balk at 'natural law'? In olden times it was easier for folk to believe in miracles, even the miracles recorded in Scripture. Then miracles were counted seals upon the record, proofs of God's greatness, Christ's divinity, a bulwark to faith. But they are not that now; indeed, they provide for many rather an obstacle to faith. The difficulty arises out of the fact that science has taught us, in these more enlightened days, that the universe is governed by natural law. And since God has given that law, some say, He cannot break it. So we cannot have miracles.

But is that really so? Must a law be broken before we can have a miracle? Surely not. And to say that God cannot intervene to alter the order of events, is to reduce Him to a weakness more puny than our own. For we can do that, and often do. We change the course of events by *using* laws of the universe, not by violating them. And if we can do that with the little handful of laws that we understand, how much more can God! Even a child knows that if he takes a handful of paper, cloth, frame-work sticks and string, and throws them up into the air, they will come down on his head, because of the law of gravitation. But if, according to another law of the universe, he fashions those same things—paper, cloth, sticks and string—into a kite, and throws them up into the air in that form, they will not fall on his head, but will fly. The shipbuilder knows as well as anyone that a lump of steel will sink—it is the law; but he also knows that if he uses another law of the universe, given by the same great Creator, and fashions his steel a certain way, that steel can be counted on to float in a great vessel. In the childhood of many of us there were no aeroplanes flying above our heads; no wireless sets in our homes, bringing us the words of people we have never seen, on the other side of the world. And what miracles medical science has presented in the same interval of time—not once, but scores of times it has happened that a living cornea has been grafted upon a sightless eye, so that the glory of shape and colour has become the lot once more of a man robbed of the precious gift of sight. And it has happened that a heart has been scraped free of harmful accretion whilst still beating, or has been massaged into activity again when it had stopped.

By now we ought to know that we cannot lightly use the word 'impossible!' If it is unwise to use that word in our own world of activity as men and women—little by little understanding the laws that God has given us—how much less should we use it when thinking of God. For the great truth is rather that this is not a world governed by law, but by God, according to law. Between the two there is a great difference. When we let ourselves sing, 'God moves in a mysterious way, His wonders to perform . . .', it can only mean mysterious to us, not to Him. Everything that exists is clear to Him. So that when it seems to His all-wise, all-loving heart, that a certain action is justified—that we men and women call a miracle—there is no reason why, in performing it, He should violate any of the laws of Nature. It is true, He may have to use laws that are as yet unknown to us.

A lot of our troubles lie in the fact that we have no really satisfactory definition of 'miracle'. 'What is a miracle?' asks Dr Edgar Dickie—and we may be glad that he asks it, because it is a question often on our lips. He answers: 'It is something which science cannot explain! A hundred years ago, if a man in Edinburgh had seen something happening at that moment in London, he would have declared: "This is a miracle!" Yet today we do not speak of television as miraculous. We might put it this way, that things go on being "miracles" for centuries, and then suddenly cease to be "miracles". It might be better, then, to alter our definition and to say, "A miracle is something which science cannot *yet* explain".'

For all that science is daily uncovering to us more of the natural laws of the universe—God's laws, and known perfectly to Him —there yet remains a great deal outside our knowledge. And always it will be so, since we cannot have knowledge equal to God.

So we are back where we started; the rose in my garden, red and fragrant and perfectly fashioned, is a miracle, since it is beyond my power to bring it forth, or to understand how it can be. And whether the time will ever come when that will not be so, I am certain that there will still be other miracles in this wonderful world in which God has set us to live. 'Life is nothing less than a standing miracle!' says Dr Haldane, bio-chemist at Cambridge. 'The Universe can be nothing less than a progressive revelation of God!' Principal W. M. Macgregor goes even a little farther: 'Miracle,' says he, 'lies very close to everyone, and beyond all gifts is the gift of open eyes to see how near it is.'

A Pocketful of Marbles

THE postman arrived this morning at morning-tea time, and my thoughts flew off in a trice to the old Sussex village of Tinsley Green. Then almost as suddenly they were off in another direction, to the happy hours of childhood.

Did you ever play marbles as a child? I did, and loved the fun of it, despite the cost later of painfully scrubbed knees, and my father's scowls as he looked at the stubbed toes of my boots.

All the boys and girls in our small country school played marbles, at the right season. We had each a print-patterned bag with a tape through the top. And we showed off our marbles, and counted them over like merchants showing off their goodly pearls. We had 'stonies'—dull little marbles that could be bought cheaply—we had 'glassies'—beautiful marbles with tiny spirals of colour in them, and some of us had super-marbles, 'blood-alleys'. The boys claimed that the little line of red in them was real blood.

We drew our rings in the playground, and carefully swept all the dust away, to leave a hard surface. Then, having placed in the ring the agreed number of our precious marbles, one by one we knelt at a distance to try to get them out—and our neighbour's, too, if possible. There were rules, of course, as unyielding as those of the Medes and Persians; but it was great fun, and sometimes we went home with a greatly increased bag, and a glow of satisfaction.

If I may say so, I was one of the best players. But for all that, I shouldn't be allowed to play today at Tinsley Green, and perhaps that is just as well, because I am not sure that my eye is as true now, or my aim with 'taw', between knuckle of bent thumb and curve of forefinger, as devastating.

The truth of the matter is that marbles at Tinsley Green is

28

not a child's game—it's a man's game. For more than three hundred and sixty years the game has been played there, and the ancient rules are still followed. So we can hardly expect any change at this late date. It all began, so an old tale says, about the time of the Spanish Armada, with a young girl, Nellie, who couldn't make up her mind which of two suitors to have. So they set their marbles in the ring, and battled it out that way.

To this day, talk around Tinsley Green at Eastertime is all of 'killers' and 'slashers' and 'terrors'. For each game, forty-nine clay marbles are cast into the ring. There are three permanent marble beds—as you will know if you have visited the village —and the championship year by year, is very earnestly contested.

As I sat over my second cup of morning tea, remembering these pleasant things, I called to mind that Heine had spoken of God the Creator as 'rattling the stars and planets in His pockets as a school-boy does his marbles. And,' said he, 'one of the pockets had a hole in it, and before God knew it, a planet slipped out and was lost. That planet was our world.'

The suggestion is striking. But surely it's a long way from the truth, for its central contention, you see, is that this is a world out of control. And despite all the muddle and suffering around, thoughtful men and women of every age have felt quite certain that that is not true. Isaiah, talking about the wonders of Creation, long before science had gone as far as it has today, long before it had given us telescopes and microscopes, once said: 'Lift up your eyes on high and see who created these?' And then he answered his own question: 'He who brings out their host by number, calling them all by name; by the greatness of His might, and because He is strong in power *not one is missing*' (Isaiah 40[26] R.S.V.).

Then one didn't get away, like a marble out of a boy's pocket with a hole in it? No, one didn't get away. This world in which we find ourselves is not a world out of control; it's not just the outcome of an accident. Isaiah was quite sure of that, and in our day men and women of the New Testament faith, and men and women of science, are even more sure of it.

To begin with, the world everywhere shows signs of being *not* an accident but an act of will—the creation of an Intelligent

29

Mind. Things fit; they have purpose and pattern. Though we have yet a lot to learn about *how* the world that is our home for a few years came into being, we have long out-grown the idea that it came into existence as the chance result of a swirling mass of atoms that jostled each other till they grouped and re-grouped. We can as little believe that the home in which we live resulted from the dumping down of a certain number of loads of stones, left to themselves, without a plan or purpose, a guiding mind and hand, a loving heart. We call that guiding hand, that loving heart, *God*: more, we call Him, *Father*. To the witness of our eyes, and of our experience, we add the witness of science, and the witness of history, and of the Scriptures. The most sceptical student of the long centuries has in the end to acknowledge that there is *something* in the rise and fall of nations that looks like 'a Power not ourselves that makes for righteousness'. 'We look back over the past,' says Professor Peake, 'and we see great empires rising, reigning, and passing. Assyria, Babylon, Persia and Rome, all of them supreme powers of the world, fell into utter ruin. And why? Because their conquests had within them the seed of their own downfall. These empires were founded on bloodshed; they had the haughtiness and pride that lead to destruction, or the luxury and vice that sap the moral stamina of the nation's life. But why should these qualities bear upon them the stamp of death? Because the Power which works in history has set its face against them, and works for righteousness.'

And to the two-fold witness of Nature and History, we add the witness of the Bible.

Tennyson might well have come from a visit to Tinsley Green —or he might have had his own, or anyone else's game of marbles in mind, when he said:

> *Ere earth gain its heavenly best,*
> *A God must mingle with the game.*

That, according to the Bible, is precisely what God the Creator of the heavens and the earth has done. That is the message of the New Testament; that is the meaning of the In-carnation: God, in His Son, born of a woman, living in an ordinary workman's home, feeling the stresses and strains of life—its joys, its hopes, its sorrows, its suffering, even death—has mingled in the game.

We have seen His Life—the graciousness of it, the courage of it, the clean, strong love of it, and His death—the cost of it—and His triumph over it, and we cannot any longer think that this is a world that doesn't matter to God any more than a marble that a boy spills accidentally. We are certain that this world is no accident, and we live seven days of the week in the faith of that mighty conviction. We say, one by one, despite all the problems:

> This is my Father's world,
>   O, let me ne'er forget
> That though the wrong seems oft so strong,
>   God is the Ruler yet.

Sunset and Sunrise

IT has been a lovely day, full of sunshine, as well as people and demands. And it closed with a Turneresque sunset.

I paused awhile at my study window; it is a gracious experience to have leisure at the end of a crowded day. It helps to get things into perspective.

In the valley below 'West Hills' was a hazy look of peace, with the odd patches of green, and trees settling comfortably for the night. The hills beyond, range upon range, were clearly outlined in diminishing tones of mauve; the sunset was mixed with a lavish hand on a palette of gold.

As I stood, the sky patterns slowly simplified, the colours losing strength. Soon only pastels and honey-gold remained; and before the odd lights came on, the whole was covered with a lightly-brushed grey, that might have clothed the breast of a dove.

It was a gracious close to a good day, and the words of the Psalmist rose to my lips: 'Praise to the Eternal's name from sunrise unto sunset!' (Psalm 113³ Moffatt). I felt the Psalmist very near. But my day was very different. He rose, as the sun rose, and went out to his shepherding, or to his tilling of the soil. The big world beyond the hills meant almost nothing to him. No wireless wakened him with a dramatic relay of the world's doings; no newspaper came to his breakfast of toast and marmalade; no postman laid a pile of letters on his desk. He was all but unaware of social obligations; no Welfare State made claims upon him; he filled in no tax-returns, to complicate his earnings and spendings. He travelled at no greater speed than his own two feet could take him, or his ass, or at best his camel. It seems incredible that he had never even heard that the earth was round, or dreamed of the law of gravitation; of steam and the combustion engine, of microbes, of vitamins; he did not even know that there was an atom, let alone an atom to be split; the magic of radium was in the world, but he didn't know of it. He knew no light but a brand from his fire, or a tiny wick in a crude clay vessel fashioned by his own hands. No one ever rang him up, or sent him a telegram; his drains never got blocked, his television mast never fouled, his 'fridge never failed. He never stretched his legs out at the day's end and relaxed, listening to a long-playing record; he never let his library book slip out of bed on to the floor, as sleep came. He never even knew that he was failing to make the best of himself—no advertisement ever told him; no psychologist ever led him down 'the labyrinthine ways' of his own mind.

And yet I know him for my kinsman. At heart, our needs are the same, and the words that rose to his lips, rise to mine, as darkness creeps over the land: 'Praise to the Eternal's name from sunrise unto sunset!'

Yet, on second thoughts, I am immensely richer than the Psalmist. He lived in the time of the Old Testament: I live in the Easter light of the New. I know, not only that the Eternal blesses me from sunrise unto sunset, but that in the realm of my spirit, where most of all I live, He turns 'my sunsets into sunrises'. That is Clement of Alexandria's way of putting it: but it's my experience. And it is something that the Psalmist never dreamed of, as he sang his praises at the day's end.

You see what it means? That every close of human experience here is linked with *a new beginning*. There are hints of it in the Old Testament, but it is never the grand certainty that it becomes in the New Testament. The world's first Easter morning changed everything. For ever now, beyond where the last sun goes down, awaits a sunrise!

The new day, to be sure, holds much of which we cannot guess. One who lived close to the Son of the Eternal who rose above the bonds of earth, and sin, on that Easter morning, put it: 'Now are we the sons of God, but it doth not yet appear what we shall be.' *What we shall be. . . .* Another, closer to us in time, has put it in contemporary terms, but with a like certainty:

33

'When I go down to the grave I can say, "I have finished my day's work", but I cannot say, "I have finished my life". My day's work will begin again next morning.'

What added praises would have risen to the lips of the Psalmist, could he have reached out to such an assurance!

A Lamp Burning Brightly

LAMPS, I know, entail a lot of work—with their constant need of oil, clean glasses, and trimmed wicks—all the same, I'm glad to have spent the nights of my childhood under the soft glow of an oil lamp. It was a magic phrase that: 'When the lamp is lit.' I heard it sometimes in the morning, sometimes late in the day, in answer to my questions. But always it was worth waiting for—that moment when, Father in from the fields and the family-circle complete, Mother set the tea, and kindled the fire, and set the lamp on the kitchen table. It was a good time of the day. The most urgent demands on my father and mother over, there would be time for answers, for reading aloud, for hand-work, for stories.

There was something primitive about lamplight; it shut out the dark world, and shut us in to ourselves in a way that the glare of electric light can never do. It was kind and friendly.

The first family to trim a lamp at nightfall must have found it much the same. The difference between our old farm kitchen and their primitive cave wouldn't be much in that moment—we both had light.

Of course, their lamp would be a simple thing of clay, fashioned by hand in the shape of a little bowl, with the rim pinched at about a third of its circumference, to keep the wick in position. As time went by, they must have discovered—in the late Canaanite, early Hebrew period—that it was a good idea to pinch it even more closely together, to form an elongated spout. Time and experience brought other minor changes. Then the closed lamp came into common use. The little bowl was covered, except for a tiny hole; then came simple ornamentation, with lines and spirals.

The discovery of a great many such lamps in the course of

Palestinian excavations, about the time I was growing up, was full of interest. In a working-man's home—the kind of home in which Jesus was a child—the lamp would be placed in a niche in the wall. Only the home of the great would boast a 'lamp-stand'.

I'm glad I grew up under the glow of a lamp, with its glass, its oil, its wick. And though our farm-house lamp must have been rather more impressive than the little pinched bowl with its oil and wick, that the prophet spoke about—a reference to Himself, that Jesus knew well—it has served all my life-long to bring me into the fellowship of lamp-users. 'Behold my Servant, whom I uphold, my chosen, in whom my soul delighteth,' he makes God to say, 'I have put my spirit upon Him. . . . He shall not cry, nor lift up, nor cause his voice to be heard in the street. A bruised reed shall he not break, and the smoking flax shall he not quench' (Isaiah 42[1-3]). It was a word of encouragement that I've never been able to do without; and it was the margin of the Revised Version that helped me to grasp it aright: 'The smoking flax' in that more accurate and meaningful version, stands as 'the dimly burning wick'.

The picture conveyed by that timely promise, of course, was of a lamp with its oil all but gone, its tiny wick needing a trim, the gusty draughts of wind or rain all but extinguishing the humble light in the darkness. It was a message that from the start must have brought encouragement and hope to those who heard it. God's Servant, His Chosen in whom His soul delighted, they were told, would be One who would understand and cherish all the hard pressed, doubtful, flickering things of the human spirit. It would be His delight to tend with loving encouragement the 'dimly burning wick', till it burned clear and full once more.

And when, in the fullness of time, men and women came near to God, in Jesus, they found Him doing exactly that—encouraging the dimly burning lamps of men's spirits.

A scornful word, a look, might have snuffed out the lamp in Peter's breast. Instead, the word that passed was: 'I have prayed for you, Peter, that your faith fail not.' For a time, Peter's lamp smouldered badly; it was a 'dimly burning wick' that all but went out. He denied his Lord, and in that denial, a cold blast from the outer spaces blew cruelly upon his little lamp. It must have looked for a time as if it would go out; but that was to forget the encouragement of Him whose ministry it was to tend 'the dimly burning wick'.

That poor wretched woman taken in adultery might easily have heard from Jesus the kind of word that would have been to her lamp as a douch of cold water. But that was not His purpose when she was dragged into His presence. And a clear flame began to burn again that day, in the poor human spirit where the wick had all but flickered out. The words she heard were: 'Go—and sin no more.' They did not spell condemnation, as she may well have expected, but encouragement.

Undoubtedly, there was something of God in such a ministry. It was more than that—though at first, those who looked upon it were surprised at its unusualness—it was *God*, reaching the deep daily needs of our human hearts.

And not for one hour has that gracious ministry ceased. Dr Maltby speaks for us today, when he says: 'In His mysterious humility, He tends the last smouldering lamp in any human heart.'

What encouragement! The cross-currents that blow so cruelly upon us are powerless against such love. The reading of the Scriptures, the silent moment of prayer, the secret piece of service, the public act of worship, He will bless. And in His mercy, He will use them, every one, to keep in our hearts a brave flame burning brightly.

A Seeker

OLD Mikimoto has died. You may not have heard. Perhaps your newspaper did not even spare space to note his passing. He was a funny old fellow. And when he died he was ninety-six; but what he did for the world was a wonderful thing. Men called him the 'Pearl King'. And he was, in a way —certainly at the end of his life he had the wealth of a king, though he had begun work at a few farthings a day.

All his life was a search. He was born in a Japanese town in the centre of the pearl industry. He grew familiar with the pearls that men knew; but always he sought a pearl above all others, round and lustrous. And always it seemed to him that it ought to be possible to speed up Nature's way of producing a pearl. That was so slow, and so much at the mercy of chance.

A grain of sand or some other foreign substance had to lodge in the oyster within the shell before the pearl could even begin. To relieve the irritation, the mollusc produced a comforting secretion, laying it over the painful foreign substance. And it went on doing this, until it attained a considerable thickness, and solidified layer by layer into a thin 'nacre'. At last, in this amazing way, an almost spherical pearl was formed. The distinctive irridescence was due partly to the content of the secretion itself, partly to the number of the very thin layers, and of course to the varying conditions of growth. And what a lovely thing was the finished pearl!

But to Mikimoto it seemed to take rather a long time. He set himself to ponder on the matter. Perhaps if Nature could be helped a little it might be a good thing; perhaps if he collected a number of oysters and prised open their shells just enough to insert a grain of sand, the result would be the same. And he set to work, speaking of his secret to no one. For three years he waited, and at the end of that time he had not produced a single pearl. His modest debts mounted, but still he had not found the lustrous pearl he sought.

Then one day all was changed. In the summer of 1893, after he had eagerly opened thousands of oyster-shells in his search, he came upon one that held a semi-circular pearl. It was not large, it was not perfect; but it pointed the way, and his search went on.

He moved next to an uninhabited island near by, that he might take advantage of an area protected from boisterous winds and tides and from enemy fish; and there he greatly enlarged his operations. Soon he had a sea-bed set out with his shells, covering seven hundred acres. Day after day he continued, tireless in his search.

In time he began to find more and more pearls, but still he was not satisfied. His search was for the perfect pearl. And at last, in 1905, he was rewarded. That find uncovered for him still another secret. All along, he had inserted the tiny piece of sand between the shell and the flesh of the oyster. But the discovery of the perfect pearl showed him plainly his mistake; the sand in the oyster that had produced the perfect pearl, was not between the shell and the oyster, but embedded in the flesh of the mullusc itself. With this discovery his search was renewed.

In time, it developed into a considerable industry; he was able to share his finds; his cultured pearls were beginning to appear in the markets where men sell pearls. At first there were protests; Mikimoto was accused of flooding the world with cheap pearls, with imitations. The protests came to a head in the court in Paris, but Mikimoto won his case—experts were able to prove that the perfect pearls he offered were completely genuine, though the old man, who had patented his secret, preferred to call them 'cultured pearls'. He had been at his search so long, that he could not imagine himself dissociated from it.

He lived a simple life, despite the great wealth that gathered around him. Modern comforts in hot weather or cold made very little appeal to him. He spent his wealth in other ways; he paid his workers well, and watched over their work and their interests like a wise father. When the Government called on the old man to invest his money in war industries, his reply was that he was a man of peace. And a man of peace he remained, dedicated wholly to his search for the great pearl. When shabby imitators flooded the markets with poor-grade pearls, he made his protests in the presence of an astonished crowd in the streets of Kobe, shovelling seven hundred and fifty thousand pearls on to a huge fire he had built. Nothing but the best was enough for Mikimoto. And no search was too long for that.

In the Gospels are two stories, one of which might have been the story of Mikimoto. Brief and beautiful, they are full of significance. Said Jesus: 'The Kingdom of heaven is like unto a treasure hidden in a field; which a man found, and hid; and in his joy he goeth and selleth all that he hath, and buyeth that field.

'Again, the Kingdom is like unto a man that is a merchant seeking goodly pearls: and having found one of great price, he went and sold all that he had, and bought it.'

There are differences in the two stories—in the one the finder stumbles upon the treasure by accident; in the other the finder of the pearl of great price is a life-long seeker. He is like Mikimoto. But the focused truth of the two stories is the same —*the Kingdom is the supreme good*.

And what our Lord is saying to those of us who would follow in His way of life is, Do you care as much as that? Is religion— the Kingdom of God, and all that is involved in it—with you, a last resort or a first priority? That is the great question.

A Word from Russia

LONG before it became possible for me to travel about the world, I fell under the spell of travel books. To this day, I have never been to Russia, but one of the earliest travel books I read was about Russia, and I have never forgotten it. Among other things that held my heart in thrall, the traveller told how he had been able to find his way through that vast country with the use of but two simple words. One was the word for 'tea', and the other was the word 'Skolko', meaning 'How much?' When he needed bread, he was able to point to the loaves that were before him in the baker's shop, and using the word 'Skolko', ask: 'How much?' When he needed lodging, as he did constantly, moving from place to place; or transport of one kind or another; or clothes, he found that the same word served.

I was struck by his simple approach to essentials. And as I pondered it, it seemed to me, as a young person, that I ought to be able to approach life with the same question. *How much*, I asked, did it cost? And *how much* ought I to offer in return?

For a long time these two questions engaged my attention; and gradually a great sense of obligation was borne in upon me; Life was very good. I accepted what each day brought; it had cost something to give it to me—my physical well-being, my home, my school, my church.

It does not surprise me now that when I was asked to prepare and give my first address, I should have chosen as my text that injunction of our Lord's, that turned on the same word, 'much'. 'Unto whomsoever *much* is given, of him shall be *much* required' (Luke 12⁴⁸).

I should have found it hard to believe that that text hung over Dr Johnson, the dictionary man, like a daily judgement: it was no judgement to me, only a daily challenge. It seemed so fair, so clear, so glorious!

I have forgotten most of what I said; I know only that I began by telling of the book I had read, and of the word with which the traveller had been able to make his way: 'Skolko', How much? It was not difficult for me, being young and newly Christian, to link it with that striking reiteration: 'Unto whomsoever *much* is given, of him shall be *much* required.' How persuasively I managed to do it I do not know, save that I faced that first company without notes—the truth so had me by the heart. And we concluded with that great hymn, 'When I survey the wondrous Cross, on which the Prince of Glory died', with its verse:

> Were the whole realm of nature mine,
> That were an offering far too small;
> Love so amazing, so divine,
> Demands my soul, my life, my all.

I wonder sometimes if this sense of obligation is as real in the experience of young Christians today—not to speak of those of us who are older—for I am certain that it must have a central and important place if life is to be good. In my own limited way, I can understand Dr Albert Schweitzer. 'One thing stirs me when I look back at my youthful days,' he says, 'the fact that so many people gave me something or were something to me without knowing it. Such people with whom I never perhaps exchanged a word, yes, and others about whom I merely heard things by report, had a decisive influence on me; they entered into my life and became powers within me. Much that I should otherwise not have felt so clearly or done so effectively was felt or done as it was, because I stand, as it were, under the sway of these people. Hence I always think that we live, spiritually, by what others have given to us in the significant hours of our life.' He has expressed his secret simply: 'Out of the depths of my feeling of happiness, there grew up gradually within me an understanding of the saying of Jesus, that we must not treat our lives as being for ourselves alone. . . .'

But none of the words of this great soul is as impressive as his life. It is life that matters most, whether one's days are spent with a stethoscope, or with a pen, or for that matter, with any other tool of this day. I love the way Winifred Holtby set it down: 'I ask that I may be permitted to love much'—there is that word again—'to serve to the utmost limit of my capacity, and to keep faith with that high vision which men call God. I shan't do it wholly. Nobody does that. I only want never to stop caring.'

Now

I HAVE just been to Synod. In his opening address, our chairman sought with some passion to underline the need for a present-day religion—one which was not a looking-back to the past, nor even a looking-on to the future. Unless our religion is something in our experience here and now, said he, it is of little value. What God did for our fathers was a glorious thing, and it is part of our heritage; but our own experience in this age must be as real, and as relevant.

As his address continued, the word Werribee kept beating its triple note in my mind. Werribee is a small place in Australia, between Melbourne and Geelong. I have been there, on a breathless, dry summer's day, my shadow at midday reduced to a purple-grey ring about my feet. But it was not of its location, temperature, or scenic attractions that I was reminded as I sat in Synod. Outside a garage in Werribee one may pause to read a notice: 'Free Petrol Tomorrow.' Of course, nobody ever gets free petrol at Werribee, because it is always promised for Tomorrow.

It shouldn't be necessary to underline such a perfectly obvious catch, yet somehow it is. We have to keep on underlining it. Arnold Bennett wrote a book: *How To Live on Twenty-four Hours a Day*. 'This day is before me,' he began, 'the circumstances of this day are my environment; they are the material out of which, by means of my brain, I have to live and be happy, and to refrain from causing unhappiness in other people. It is the business of my brain to make use of this material. My brain is in its box for this sole purpose. Not tomorrow! Not next year! But now! Today, exactly as today is!'

That, in the realm of religion, was our chairman's emphasis. A notice that offers free petrol tomorrow is no good, nor is a religion that offers happiness tomorrow, or power tomorrow; the recurring note in the New Testament is *Now*!

It is a stimulating exercise to take up a concordance, and note the fact. A good beginning faces one in the question of Jesus: 'Do ye *now* believe?' (John 16[31]). And the record of the early Christian Church is as challenging. Those who entered into the Christian experience in those tremendous days had, in many cases, no past to look back to, and no certainty of any future. They lived in the present—in the Now. Times were difficult, but their religion was adequate. 'Many Christians today talk about "the difficulties of our times",' says J. B. Phillips, 'as though we should have to wait for better ones before the Christian religion can take root. It is heartening to remember that this faith took root and flourished amazingly in conditions that would have killed anything less vital in a matter of weeks. Those early Christians were on fire with the conviction that they had become through Christ, literally sons of God; they were pioneers of a new humanity, founders of a new Kingdom. Perhaps if we believe what they believed, we might achieve what they achieved.' The secret of that vital religion that changed their lives, and that of the age in which they lived, lay in that little word 'now'. See how it recurs all through the shining record: '*Now* being made free from sin, and become servants of God, ye have your fruit unto holiness, and the end everlasting life', or as J. B. Phillips puts it even more tellingly: '*Now* that you are employed by God, you owe no duty to sin, and you reap the fruit of being made righteous, while at the end of the road there is Life for evermore.' Whether one chooses the Authorized Version or the translation by Phillips, one sees the Christian lifting his eyes only for a moment to scan the horizon; his great moment is *now*—*now* provides the setting in which his new life in God is operative. '*Now* is the accepted time, behold *now* is the day of salvation,' says Paul to the Corinthians (2 Corinthians 6[2]). '*Now* are ye full, *now* are ye rich,' the Christians in Rome are reminded (Romans 4[5]). And to this, Paul adds his own witness: 'The life which I *now* live in the flesh, I live by faith in the Son of God, who loved me, and gave Himself for me' (Galatians 2[20]). Other writers give the same emphasis. '*Now* we see not yet all things put under Him, but we see Jesus' (Hebrews 2⁸⁻⁹). 'Beloved, *now* are we the sons of God, and it doth not yet appear what we shall be' (1 John 3²). 'Now' is the recurring note; and it is the sure mark of all valid Christian experience.

Coleridge puts it well:

> Think not the faith by which the just shall live
> Is a dead creed, a map correct of heaven,
> Far less a feeling, fond and fugitive,
> A thoughtless gift, withdrawn as soon as given;
> It is an affirmation and an act
> That bids eternal truth be present fact.

Who wants free petrol tomorrow? What's the use of religion that is only operative in the future? What's wrong with Here and Now? If God is almighty, all-wise and all-loving, surely He does not need certain circumstances to be present before He can act. If the response to Himself which He has quickened in your spirit and mine is real religion, then surely it is relevant today. If it is good then it is good Here and Now.

Growing Up

I HAVE just waved off some friends on their way to London. They are full of eagerness.

One of the most surprising rewards of travel is the pleasure of recognition. I discovered it when I first made a visit to the great, grey beauty of London, and through the ethereal haze of the embankment saw the figure of Big Ben, and found he was just as I expected him to be; and I discovered it when I saw for the first time Barrie's immortal Peter Pan in Kensington Gardens, and found he was just as I expected him to be.

Barrie had just died, and the little children who played about Peter Pan, under the care of their nannies, had put a garland of flowers about him. But there he stood, just as Sir George Frampton had set him down, in his green corner overlooking the Long Water. There, from his sculptured tree-stump, he lifted up his pipe of music, whilst a fairy tip-toed at his feet, in company with a squirrel and a number of bunnies.

I had no need to urge my friends to see Big Ben as soon as they get to London—they can hardly miss him; but a little effort is required to seek out Peter Pan. With his slender boyish form, and his little pipe up-lifted, he is a delight. But from what a friend—lately returned—tells me, it would seem that at least one person in the world has never heard of him. Consulting her map and guide-book, my friend found herself at a loss; either trees blocked her view, or she hadn't walked far enough. So she intercepted a passer-by. 'Excuse me,' queried my friend, 'have you seen Peter Pan? Isn't he just round about here?'

'I dunno,' came the surprising reply. 'Why, 'ave yer lost 'im?'

It would be a pity to lose that delightful little figure, though it would be a good thing if some of us could lose our Peter

Pannishness; the attitude to life of the little boy who would not grow up.

There is no question about our growth in body; from the time of Mother Eve—coaxing her two lads—to this day, every mother knows the secret: 'Come, eat it up, it will make you grow!' Our greatest desire is to grow; our proudest moments are when buttons are let out, and hems let down. There is an old saying: 'You've got to do your own growing, no matter how tall your grandfather was.' The time comes when the pencil-marks, creeping up inch by inch on the door-post no longer register growth. From now on, growth is a matter of mind and spirit. Exams serve to mark mental growth for a while; successive rises in wages, and increasing responsibility in work, are other tests. But that is not all.

And because it is not all, there is an inescapable challenge in the conversation between a mother and child that came to my notice recently: 'Mother, do you still grow?'

Replied the mother, as she faced that question:

'I let the measuring rod
Slip closer to my child's head. . . .
Three foot two . . .

Do I still grow?
Do I still grow?
This afternoon I suffered
From unkind words
But smiled.
Last year I would have been
Quite proud
Of making sharp retort.
Last week I set aside
My own desires
For others!
Last year I would have cried:
"I'll have my way,
Let others yield to me."
Last month I found some beauty

48

In a soul once scorned,
And told it to another.
Do I still grow?

Yes, child,
But oh, so slowly . . .'

Yet grow one must. St Peter, who knew the hard inner meaning of his words more than most of us—having stumbled so badly—wrote: 'Grow: grow in grace, and in the knowledge of our Lord and Saviour Jesus Christ.' Grace and knowledge—how fitting they are when coupled. Yet how Peter Pannish many of us are!

J. M. Barrie, who gave us the figure of Peter Pan, is remembered to have said: 'The God to whom little boys say their prayers, has a face very like their mother's.' That may be so; but the God to whom big boys, and young men and women and the rest of us say our prayers, ought to have a face very different from our mother's!

In the story of the race, the conception of God began very simply. That is part of the fascination of the early pages of Scripture; they belong to a child-people—a child-people set on growth. At first, they are satisfied to think of God as One who walks in the garden at the close of day. For a long time their conception of Him continues almost as simple; they think of Him as localized in one special place, Mount Sinai; as having a face like a man, and using hands, and sometimes even showing His back. But those ideas grew—they had to. In time, Isaiah spoke of Him as a God of Holiness, and in his turn Amos spoke of Him as a God of Judgement; and Hosea came forward to share an even larger idea, that He was a God of Mercy. Holiness, Judgement, Mercy! The conception of God in the hearts of men was growing. Then came the revelation of God that Jesus brought; that above all, He was Father!

It is not easy to escape that penetrating question: 'Do I still grow?' When I think of God, is it in the childish way in which I thought of Him as a child? Or is it in one of the partial ways men thought of Him in the childhood of the race? Or is it in

49

the light of the New Testament revelation of Jesus? *Do I still grow?*

Dr James Reid sums it up: 'Till the "soul wakes and grows", however well the physical and mental part of us may have grown, our true development is arrested. We are spiritual defectives. . . . It is childish, for instance, to find our chief rest and seek our happiness in things. Again, it is childish to be unduly sensitive to the hurts that others may do to us, and to be easily resentful of criticism, or even of opposition. It springs from pride, of course, from a good conceit of ourselves. But it is a relic of childhood. It is rooted in the desire to stand well with others, and perhaps in a sense of inferiority that makes us feel the need to be encouraged and sustained by their good opinion. The grown-up way of meeting the slings and arrows of criticism is to realize that no one can really hurt us except ourselves. If we are wrong, it is good to be made aware of it, however humbling. If we are right, the person who attacks or criticizes does us no real harm.'

The question that I have to ask myself in the secret places is: Am I growing up in my day-to-day relationships with people?—in my respect for them, and their opinions, and their right to hold them?—in my readiness to give and take?—in my knowledge of, and responsibility toward, the world family? Am I growing in my stewardship of things, of money, of strength, of time?

Am I really growing in the grace and knowledge of Jesus Christ?

For Dear Life

MELINDA RANKIN was a valiant soul. There was something ageless about Melinda, though, as her name suggests, she belonged to last century. She kept hearing things about life in Mexico that troubled her. And straightway she felt something ought to be done about it. She knocked on the door of her minister. 'Is this right,' she asked, 'this superstition, this religious ignorance?' Then she sought out the elders in the congregation. She wrote to the leaders of the denomination. 'But we are not listening', their actions said, if not their words. 'There is no money! It is too far away! Nobody is prepared to go! The job is impossible!'

Then said Melinda: 'God helping me, I will go myself.' And she did. When the incredibly hard journey was behind her, she found she was not allowed to enter Mexico. So she settled meanwhile in two bare rooms in a town just across the border.

At long last, she was allowed to cross over into Mexico. And she established the first Protestant Church there with a hundred and seventy members. It was no easy task. She was driven from door to door. If she was blocked in one direction, she sat down and thought out a new plan. Describing her life, she said an unforgettable thing in a letter written to the home church: 'The word discouragement is not in the dictionary of the Kingdom of Heaven.'

And that's as true now as ever—but that word is in the dictionary of the kingdoms of earth.

A legend says that one day the Devil put up his tools for sale. One after another they were displayed, and one after another disposed of. To everybody's surprise, the tool that occasioned most interest, and brought the highest price, was a dull-edged tool. Answering questions as to why that was, the Devil had to admit that it was his most valuable tool—*the tool of Discouragement!*

If you have felt its dull, deadening blows—and who among us has not?—sit down, when you have a minute to call your own, and read the third chapter of the New Testament letter to the Colossians. It's the most practical thing I know. It's all about husbands and wives, and servants and children. And it has a special word for fathers. I think that must be because in the set-up of those days, fathers had almost unlimited power over those of their household. It's not very long, for that matter, since Stopford Brooke wrote, with some feeling: 'I have no patience with those fathers'—and he added 'mothers' as well—'who make of their children's sense of duty to them a daily scourge for the backs of their children, and deliberately forget and ignore that they have a duty to their children.'

Well, there have been changes. The apostle who wrote that letter to the Colossian households might be astonished to find how much hard fatherly authority and discipline has been slackened in our day. But still, I believe, he would want that word to stand: 'Fathers, provoke not your children, that they be not discouraged.'

In this modern day, I see no good reason why this word should be restricted to fathers; I feel it ought to include mothers and teachers and all the rest of us. And I see no good reason why it should be restricted to children—for we all know the deadly bludgeoning of that Devil's tool, discouragement. Children and young people, of course, are specially susceptible; and that's what the apostle has in mind. What he is saying—and how surprising it must have sounded when he set it down—is that even the youngest have rights. Authority and discipline—good things both of them—are not in question, save where they are blunderingly used to an unhappy end. The danger of over-stepping the mark in harshness and injustice is not very real these days; though constant interference and fault-finding can provoke to discouragement. But that is not all. Day by day, indifference to spiritual values in relationships in the home, the school, the business, can lead to the same end, discouragement. It is impossible in youth, or indeed at any other time, to live fully in a God-rejecting atmosphere.

It is a responsibility too great for human bearing—the use of this Devil's tool when dealing with the young—and every day there is the temptation, in our homes, our classes, our clubs, our places of business. B. K. Cunningham of Westcott House, Cambridge, underlines this with all the power at his command. He tells us of a boy whose form-master interrogated him as to his intended career. 'Others had already been asked round the form and had given their answers. When it came his turn, the lad screwed up his courage and replied: "A clergyman, sir!" The form-master ejaculated contemptuously: "A clergyman! You're more fitted to be a barman." The lad,' added Cunningham, 'by the grace of God, managed to get out, "Sir, you're a cad", and burst into tears.' Telling of it, B. K. Cunningham added quietly: 'I know that is true, for I was that boy.' Sarcasm, injustice, impatience, indifference! Whilst that tool of the Devil's is cruellest of all to youth, it's cruel to any.

Melinda Rankin's words remain true: 'Discouragement does not belong to the Kingdom of Heaven.' *But Encouragement does!* And what a sharp and shining tool that is, unlocking possibilities, strengthening the feeble knees, quickening the faint-hearted. If you and I have a word of encouragement to give, we ought to give it where it will count. None of us can get on without encouragement. Those among us who are by nature self-distrustful need it especially; those who face a new, a dull, or a difficult task need it especially; those who live weighted with heavy responsibility for others need it especially. We'll have opportunities this day. Let us take a word of encouragement, and use it where it will count!

Is Prayer for Bread a Farce?

THE first 'strong crust of friendly bread' that I knew was my mother's loaf, as she lifted it from the oven and set it to cool on a folded linen cloth. It was golden brown, wholesome, and as sweet smelling as the new day. And when later we cut it into great slices, how good it was!

So the petition of the Lord's Prayer that I learned in childhood, and have repeated ever since, has always seemed to me close to life: 'Give us this day our daily bread.'

There was work to keep father in the fields all the year round. In the hottest time of the year, which brought harvest, we children joined him. We helped with stooks, carried out cool drinks, and chased the harvest mice. Then, at the end of autumn, we gathered with our hardworking elders in chapel, and sang our harvest hymns, and gave thanks to God that 'all was safely gathered in'.

It seemed to us the most natural thing that the preacher should look down to us from a pulpit surrounded with sheaves and garlanded with grapes, and that the central place that day should be taken by a great golden loaf. Pumpkins and marrows, rosy apples, quinces and nuts were there, too—of the bounty of harvest. And never once did we neglect to place there a glass of clear, cool water. We knew—none better—how much we depended on the rain that God sent upon the just and the unjust. We knew how little we could do without it, and how powerless we were to regulate it. We knew and laughed at the story of the old Methodist farmer who prayed in a time of drought, and more earnestly when weeks of hot sun gave way to a sudden and continuous downpour: 'Dear Lord, last week we axed 'ee vur rain. And when we axed 'ee vur rain dear Lord, us wanted dapper little

54

showers like. But, O Lord, this is ridiklus.' Had the management of the weather been in our hands, we might have been as little satisfied; happily it wasn't, so we gave our energies to ploughing, cultivating, sowing and the hot work of harvesting. It did not seem to us unfitting to bow our heads to pray, 'Give us this day our daily bread', or once a year, at harvest's end, to carry our sheaves into chapel, and sing our harvest hymns. We knew we were dependent on the mercies of God.

I was shocked to read lately in a report to a commission of the British Council of Churches: 'The farmer of today knows how to get good crops without praying over them.'

Does that mean that agricultural science has robbed us of the simple sincerity of harvest thanksgiving? that our human dependence has become smothered under the achievements of chemical fertilizers? that we have lost our way among tractors turned out in their thousands from the production-line of great factories?

It is true that many of us today live divorced from the countryside; our bread comes to us morning by morning for a few pence, over a shop-counter, or from a van delivering at our gate. It takes an effort to cast ourselves back to the realism of the verse that once everyone who ate bread understood well:

> Back of the loaf is the snowy flour,
> And back of the flour is the mill,
> And back of the mill is the sun and shower,
> And the wheat, and the Father's will.

The appearance of things—as the report to the commission suggests—seems to make a fool of that kind of thinking. But may it not be the other way round?

Of what use is the plough drawn efficiently over the countryside by a powerful tractor, the fertilizer developed in the laboratory, the uncanny skill of the binder and thresher, the baker's belonging to the right union, if the ancient gifts of soil, sun and rain are withheld? And whose gifts are they? They are the gifts of God who made them—and us—and called us into partnership. However much we pride ourselves on our modern mechanisms, we still depend for our very life on God-given bread. The setting, of course, is different, but the truth that Augustine saw still remains: 'Without God, we cannot. Without us, God will not.'

However modern our techniques, there is no contracting out of that relationship; we are dependent. That is the first reality of Harvest Thanksgiving.

And the second is like unto it: as we bow daily to pray, 'Give us this day our daily bread', we know ourselves not only bound to God in the production of our harvest, but bound to our fellow-men the world over in the enjoyment of it. Nicolas Berdyaev is right—and he is not talking of a life long ago and far away; he is talking of our world here and now—when he says: 'The question of bread for myself is a material question, but the question of bread for my neighbour, for everybody, is a spiritual and religious question.'

How different things would be if we realized it. All the time, of course, the Prayer we pray is not 'My Father . . .' but '*Our* Father, give *us* this day *our* daily bread'. Because so many of us have failed to recognize this, we find ourselves in a frightening world today, with waste in parts, and extreme want in others. Not that there is any shortage of bread. God has set within the framework of seasons, showers, sun and in-gatherings, ample for His children's needs; but only on one daring assumption, that we shall live together as One Family. And just at this point our economy breaks down, because our religion breaks down. It is at this point that the Communist finds his chance today; between the selfish, uneasy fear of the 'Haves', and the hungry bitterness of the 'Have-Nots'.

We have at least two lessons to learn yet, before our world will come right.

The Magic Atom

PEACEFUL use of the atom now matters to us all a great deal. Three times a day I have occasion to think of the Atom man. I don't think of him that often, though I can never forget in this amazing century the importance of being Ernest Rutherford. The silver serviette-ring that lies beside my plate at table is one of a pair given by Lord Rutherford's parents to my parents at the time of their marriage. My father and Ernest were cousins. They were born within a stone's throw of each other in Nelson. Ernest's home was a modest shingle-roofed house at Spring Grove, with which I was familiar most of my childhood. But I did not meet him until he visited us, when he returned as an eminent physicist, to deliver the Cawthron Institute Lecture. He was good enough to give me a ticket for his lecture.

And in 1937, when I made my first visit to England, I packed away in my luggage a photograph I had taken of the old Spring Grove house, that he was anxious to have. But I was never able to give it to him in person. We corresponded, and I was to have visited him at Cambridge, but before that I had to make a trip to the Continent. And it so happened, that the very first newspaper placard that met my gaze at the docks on my return that autumn afternoon, bore the brief tidings: 'Greatest British Scientist Dead.' It was Ernest Rutherford.

A day or two later I stood in Westminster Abbey, to represent the family at the funeral of New Zealand's greatest son. He was laid to rest in that quiet place beside the immortal Sir Isaac Newton. 'With the death of Rutherford,' said one, 'a great epoch in science came to an end—Rutherford was the Newton of the atom.' Lord Baldwin said of him: 'His refreshing personality, his dauntless spirit, the merry twinkle of his eye, the exuberance of his ever-youthful enthusiasm . . . one can only say he was a man, a peer among men: he was Rutherford.'

And men are still paying him tributes, tributes that in this age of the magic atom are beginning at last to get into true focus. Up till now, a certain terror has attached itself to the gift he was able to make to the world when he split the atom—and that is understandable, when we remember that the first time his wonderful secret was used was at Hiroshima, to destroy, instead of to serve life. He was a man of peace all his days, and it is not difficult to picture his distress at such an order of things.

But now that distinguished scientists have gathered at Geneva, to pool their atom knowledge for peaceful purposes, the contribution that Ernest Rutherford made is seen by common people in a new light. Sir John Cockcroft—the Director of British Atomic research, who as a young man worked with Rutherford—assures us that we are at last on the doorstep of a new day. And Dr Niels Bohr, the eminent Danish scientist and Nobel Prize winner, hastens to underline the importance of this new move. Inaugurating a series of public lectures on the peaceful uses of the atom, he paid tribute to Rutherford. 'The development of modern atomic science,' said he, 'is the outcome of a most intense international co-operation, in which the progress has been so rapid and the intercourse so intimate that it is often impossible to disentangle the contribution of individuals to the common enterprise. I shall abstain from mentioning names of living scientists, but I feel that we are united in paying tribute to the memory of Ernest Rutherford, who with such vigour explored the new field of research opened by the great discoveries of Roentgen, Thomson, Becquerel, and the Curies. We think not only of Rutherford's fundamental discoveries of the atomic nucleus and its transmutability, but above all of the inspiration with which, through so many years, he guided the development of this new branch of physical science.'

Then he went on to underline the grave responsibility resting on scientists today, to use and not abuse this mighty secret that could as easily destroy as serve our civilization.

As a young man, with the first glow of fame upon him, Ernest is remembered to have said, that but for gaining a scholarship

A MIRACLE

to Nelson College he might have been a farmer all his days, and never realized his special gifts.

It is of interest to know something of his simple home background. By the time little Ernest was ready for school, his family moved from Spring Grove to Foxhill, where his father, Mr James Rutherford, was soon engaged in milling and farming. With brothers and sisters and chests and bedding and the grandfather-clock all piled into the four-horse wagon, it must have been a memorable day for Ernest—his first move from his birthplace. He was to make many, and much longer journeys as the years went by. Foxhill proved a good place in which to be a boy with a lively mind. There was the little school, and the farm and orchard, and the river. And every now and again Newman-and-Holder's coaches pulled in to make a stop on their journey. There were young things on the farm, calves and pigs; and Ernest, along with his brothers, had to take a share in looking after them. On Saturday afternoons in the spring, there was bird-nesting; and in the summer, there were other ploys. There were no organized games at the little school—the boys organized their own. Mental arithmetic at school, and the homework that Mother set, seemed to Ernest as good as a game. Mother had been a teacher at Spring Grove before her marriage, and she was one who valued education for her family. During those same days as a schoolmistress, she had saved to buy a cherished Broadwood piano; and she loved to gather her family around her at Foxhill, to sing old songs and hymns on Sunday evenings, Father playing his violin.

The great outside world at that time made little impact on the family. In time, Ernest went off to Nelson College; and Nelson College is proud to remember him today. A little beyond the main entrance is the Rutherford Collection—the spectacles through which he peered at calculus and formulae, the tobacco-pouch into which he dipped much later in his career, as he pondered the mysteries of radioactivity, some of his early report cards and scholarship papers. Nelson College boys of this Age of the Atom may be forgiven if they pick out a sentence from one of those old reports with some amusement. It reads: 'A very good boy from whom one may look for good results.' That was in 1889, Ernest's last year at Nelson.

In a short time he was off to Canterbury University College, leaving his Principal and Masters at Nelson a little mystified. He had won three prizes and was top of the sixth form in all subjects. 'Unbelievable' was the word they used. It was obvious that he must go on to Canterbury.

That was the beginning of Ernest's life in the bigger world. Soon it was Cambridge University, then McGill, then Manchester—and back to Cambridge, where he directed a physical laboratory for nearly forty years.

But he never forgot Nelson. When he lay dying in his home in Cambridge, he remembered to tell his wife that he wished to leave a gift of a hundred pounds to his old College—Nelson. Those were, as it proved, almost his last words. But he left much more—to Nelson a proud name, and to the world a great secret—only now are we beginning to know how great.

Two Words

LATELY I shared a cup of tea in a sunny window with a retired hospital sister. She is crippled now, but she served to the end of the war. The latter part of her ministry was in the old people's wards, and she told me one or two very human stories.

One night, an old man who thought he was dying called to her: 'Sister, could you say a prayer with me? Do you know one? Isn't there one called "The Lord's Prayer"?'

Yes, there was: and Sister said it with him that night, and again the next and the next. It is a good prayer to die with—but above all, it is a good prayer to live with. See how it starts: 'Our Father . . .' When our Lord set those words upon the lips of those who asked Him how to pray, He gave them not only comfort, but an infinite challenge.

St Teresa is said to have spent an hour over those two opening words; and well she might. No other form of words has such a hold upon mankind. They are taught to little children; they are a challenge when the sun is high, they are a comfort to the aged when the shadows fall; they are known and used by the whole Church the world round; they are part of every set service from baptism to burial; they form the very heart of private prayer. People who differ in many ways, come together in the use of those words that belong to all the Father's children: 'Our Father . . .'

If Jesus had not told us that this was what God is like, we could hardly have dared believe it, for it is an altogether startling and presumptuous thing for any one of us mortal creatures to address the almighty, eternal, holy God as 'Our Father'. But He did much more than tell us this, He lived it—till now, what He has told us, and what He has shown us, persuade us utterly.

The word 'Father', of course, is used of God in various ways. In the Old Testament, He is many times referred to as the Father of the nation of Israel. Again, in the New Testament—in the passages in John 14, and in chapter 17—He is spoken of as the Father of Jesus, in a sense in which He is not the Father of us all. Yet again, in the Sermon on the Mount, He is referred to as the Father of all men. And last of all, the name is used—in its highest and greatest sense—to denote the relationship of God to all believers. It is in this fourth, precious sense that Jesus used the word in this great prayer; it speaks of a spiritual relationship. The prayer was not given to the crowds who clamoured for healing or for the loaves and fishes, but to those who in their inmost hearts stood in a new relationship with God. And when we use those great words, we use them in this sense.

We also presuppose that there is a family—a number of people who stand in the same relationship to the Father; and that we belong to that family. This is a very wonderful thing indeed, and when it dawns upon us, three lovely things are quickened within us—a sense of belonging; a sense of enrichment; and inevitably, a sense of obligation.

First, there is our sense of belonging—our sense of belonging to God, and to countless others in all the earth, by faith. And what is more wonderful? I can remember when it first dawned upon me. I was leading a service in a tiny chapel in the south of England. It was in an international camp, and we had there Christians from eleven different countries; but it was most wonderful when we joined in that great prayer that our Lord gave us, each in her own tongue, so that a girl from Germany prayed, not 'My Father', but 'Our Father', and a girl from Czechoslovakia prayed not 'My Father', but 'Our Father . . .' and a girl from Holland prayed 'Our Father', and girls from England, from Ireland, from Switzerland, from New Zealand —each prayed 'Our Father'. I've had other and similar experiences since—in a great international service of youth in St Martin-in-the-Fields, London, when for a moment I lifted my eyes to glimpse those kneeling beside me; again in a world conference communion Sunday at Oxford, when I took upon my lips those words, after I had knelt beside a Nigerian Christian as black as a velvety night, an Indian in a bright sari, beyond her a modern American, on the other side an English friend; and we had taken the sacred elements from Bishop Sommer of Germany.

Never now, when I use those words, 'Our Father', can I escape this wonderful sense of belonging, this sense of enrichment, and this sense of obligation. This is where the prayer's challenge to life comes in. Whatever comfort this great prayer has for the dying, there is no escaping its challenge to those of us who live.

We pray 'Our Father which art in Heaven'; and when we do that in any real sense, we feel obliged to look around and say, 'Our brothers and sisters which are on earth'. There is no escape. Our brother is that Indian bereft of food; our brother is that African bereft of justice; our brother is that Maori youth, who walks the way to school, to work with us; our brother is that old pensioner sitting lonely in his little room in the city; our brother is every one who takes upon his lips those same words—'*Our* Father . . .'

To See the End

LITTLE Jack London wasn't yet nine, and his work was to sit under a tree from sunrise to sunset and watch the bees. As he waited for the swarming, he had plenty of time to read. But that blessed state was aggravated by the fact that he had only one book—and the last chapters of that were missing. He read it avidly through the long summer hours, and re-read it; but he never got to know the end of the story—until years later, when he was able to lay hands on another copy.

It is hard to imagine anything more frustrating—to be young, to have lots of time, to have a book, and then never to know how it ends.

When in 1935, Jane Addams, that wonderful founder of Hull House, Chicago, was confronted with the operation, which proved to be her last, she begged first for time to finish the book she was reading; she wanted so much to know 'how it would end'.

And that is something that we all want to know—of a good book, a story, an experience—and to be cheated is more than we can bear.

Have you noticed those four striking words in Matthew's account of the trial of our Lord? (Matthew 26⁵⁸). Things had taken a dramatic turn. Jesus had been betrayed, and in a matter of moments made a prisoner and led away. Scattered in fear, His disciples let Him go; 'but Peter followed Him afar off unto the High Priest's palace . . . to see the end.'

To see the end? The end of Jesus, the end of that lovely, courageous life, the end of those gracious acts, those miraculous cures, the end of all those stories to which the common people had listened gladly, the end of all their hopes? The end of everything? To Peter's shocked, bewildered heart it certainly looked like it.

But however much it looked like it, of course, Peter was wrong—gloriously wrong. And he was one of the first to know it on that never-to-be-forgotten morning when the stone was rolled away, and the message was: 'Go tell His disciples, and Peter.'

In no time, a little company in that same city where Peter had moved with lagging steps to see the end of his Lord were claiming that He was alive; more, that they had seen Him, felt Him, heard Him. And the greater number who could know the wondrous truth the better—there was no point in waiting till the news had become dulled at the edges, till those who had been officially involved in the tragedy of the Cross were comfortably out of the way, till they had forgotten how passionately they had pursued it. The end, it had to be admitted, was so utterly unlike anything Peter and his friends had ever dreamed, that one of their number had even refused to believe it when attested by his trusted friends.

What had been feared to be the end was soon seen to be but the beginning. Scattered to the far corners of the earth by persecution, Peter and his friends went everywhere preaching the resurrection of their Lord—their despair replaced with certainty, their gloom with gladness. With the passing of the years, their numbers were augmented, though the course of the new life was never anything but dangerous. Some were banished from kinsfolk, some were thrown to the lions, some were smeared with pitch to become torches to add a festive note to Nero's games. But no danger could stop them. Pilate was forgotten, and Nero, and Diocletian, but not the living Christ; rather were men and women reminded of the word which had preceded His birth: 'Thou shalt call His name Jesus . . . and of His Kingdom there shall be no end.'

Of course, we are often like Peter. We look out on to some sudden event that comes crowding into our days, and it seems the very end of things. There is nothing new in that. Since the days of Peter, men and women who have cared greatly for the Kingdom of Peter's Lord have registered moments of despair, as well as moments of steady faith. 'I can compare the condition of the Church at this epoch,' said Bishop Lightfoot, in the tenth century, 'to nothing else but the fate of the prisoner in the story as he awakens to the fact that the walls of his iron den are closing in on him, and shudders to think of the inevitable end.'

It is a long way from Peter to the tenth century, and from the tenth century to our own twentieth century; but during the whole of that time the Church has had its Peters. Nor are they lacking among spokesmen of our day who make no pretence to follow Peter's Lord. 'The end of everything is at hand', was H. G. Wells's parting message. 'There is no way out, or round or through the impasse. It is the end. Our universe is not merely bankrupt, it is going clear out of existence. The attempt to trace a pattern of any kind is absolutely futile.'

But Peter's living Lord remains, unchanged—'Jesus Christ, the same yesterday, today and for ever.'

Luggage

WE are born, it seems, with a craze for luggage. I think of it every time I come back from seeing a friend off by ship or train. Only when I'm travelling myself—with my own all about me, and not a minute to give to anything else—am I spared this clear judgement.

'Has it ever struck you,' asks Helen Wilson in her pioneer story, *My First Eighty Years*, 'that handy little suitcases are a modern invention? Our grandparents travelled with chests, large or not so large, or with cardboard boxes, unashamed. Remember the old lady who, anxious to lose none of her things, kept repeating the inventory throughout the journey: "Big box, little box, hand-box, bundle"!'

My hope is that our need to travel by air will teach us to travel light; but it's not so easy as it seems. The climate is the trouble —one day it's hot, the next it's cold. To dash off for a week-end is one thing—ten miles or a hundred and ten—though I'm always surprised that one needs nearly as many things for a week-end as for a week. A change of clothes is, of course, essential—a cake of soap, a tooth-brush and a few other toilet needs—and it's usually necessary to poke in an umbrella or a coat, or both. Even the lightest dressing-gown, added to one's night attire, seems to take up an unaccountable lot of space. And if it is winter-time, there is no shame in casting a glance at one's old stand-by, the hot-water bottle hanging on the back of the bathroom-door. If one is sure of the habits of one's hostess, this can be left at home—on a second visit, anyway. But a warm, comfortable sleep is an important part of an absence from home. And it seems impossible to travel decently without some sort of shoe-cleaning outfit; as it is impossible to travel without a handbag for tickets and money, and a book for the journey.

And I must confess I would as soon think of travelling without a note-pad and pen and pencil, as without a cake of soap or a dab of powder for a shiny nose. Then there are times when it would seem as much a folly to leave one's old camera at home—and little odd-shaped boxes of film have to be stowed in somewhere against the awkwardness of coat-hangers and the heels of shoes. So the story goes on.

When it is not a matter of a mere week-end, but of months, then it's more serious. 'I live in a suitcase,' says Margaret Mackay, in her light-hearted book of that title; and it seems that we are to hear a word of hope from one who has broken through this age-old servitude to luggage. But is it so? 'Wandering abroad for months at a time,' she begins, with scarcely more signs of enlightenment than the rest of us, 'one needs rather a variety of clothes—for cold weather and hot weather, for city and country, for street and sport, and evening. Since it is somehow a loss to Travel Heavy, I struggle to Travel Light. But if you are away for nearly a year'—and how well she speaks to my condition—'this proves more expensive in the long run than Travelling Heavy, because you are eventually forced to replace certain things which you have left behind . . . an extra sweater, a bathing-suit, a reference book, a blouse when the laundry is late. Furthermore, to hold these unscheduled additions you are obliged to buy another inexpensive little zip-bag—and in the next country you can never find anything to match the bag you bought in the one before.' The idea is just to stow in the temporary overflow; but it never works out like that. 'So,' adds this experienced globe-trotter, 'though I started out long ago with everything neatly uniform, after years of travelling in many lands, I find my luggage would look most appropriate perched on top of a gipsy's caravan.'

Erik Routley reminds us that when our Lord sent out His first disciples, two by two, 'He emphasized the necessity of travelling light'. They were to take nothing save a staff; no script, no bread, no money; and they were to be shod with sandals, and not bother even about a second coat. It is easy to point out that they had many advantages over those of us who travel today; but is this word of wisdom from the first century of our faith to be so easily set aside? Is there not something in it more penetrating than most of us are ready to admit?

Is it not true that we modern disciples are far too addicted to luggage—to carrying in the centre of our lives, things: not to mention fears, grudges, and solid chunks of pride? Why do we do it? Is it because we are not sure of ourselves? If we were as sure of our Lord—and of ourselves—as those first-century disciples, perhaps we could afford to travel this human way much less encumbered.

The Face All-glorious

ON my study wall, just above eye-level, as I look up from my desk, is a miniature of that lovely picture of Sallman's of the Face all-glorious. 'Do you really think He looked like that?' asked a friend. Well, who can tell?

Of her lover, Prue Sarn set down these things: 'How did he look? What was he like? Was he well-favoured? It be hard to say. There be no looks in love, no outward seeming, no telling over of features.' When we think of our Lord, we find these same questions rising in our hearts: 'How did He look? What was He like? Was He well-favoured?'

Strangely, those who have told us all we know of His thoughts, His deeds, and the spirit of Him—Peter, Mark, John and the others—spared not a sentence in their gospels to tell us how He looked. Perhaps Prue Sarn's word is the right one: 'There be no looks in love, no outward seeming, no telling over of features.

The earliest 'portraits' we have of our Lord fall within the first five centuries, and vary greatly, according to the mood and temper of the time. The first shows Him a youthful bearded figure—setting forth, in classical form, perfect humanity. The second school of portraiture represents Him bearded and strong—a man of the class, and of the geographical setting to which he belonged. And later as monastic and ascetic trends became more widely felt, the portrayal of Him became more severe, and he was shown with long hair and purposeful eyes. It is difficult to tell which of these, if any, gave a real representation of Him.

'Many reasons have been adduced,' a modern artist says, 'for the absence of any authentic contemporary portrait; it is probably sufficient explanation to recall that none of the apostles and disciples (themselves unportrayed and undescribed) thought

it necessary to mention even in passing the appearance of Christ.'
Life, as they saw it, was largely a matter of spirit. All the
'portraits' of Christ that we have, therefore, are imaginary, and
date from long after His death.

The earliest *word*-picture we have belongs to the letters of
Lentulus, written in the twelfth century, though based on
writings of a much earlier period. His description of our Lord
was of one tall, finely proportioned, with hair the colour of
wine, and a forked beard. His face, Lentulus claimed, was
ruddy and slightly oval, His forehead clear and without lines.
His mouth faultless, His eyes brilliant and awe-inspiring, blue
in colour and flashing. His whole countenance, he claimed,
impressed beholders with fear and love. In speech, He was
gentle; in teaching, full of seriousness and grace.

Other writers who came a little later spoke of His eyes as
'tawny', but perhaps both portrayals were affected by the mood
of the time. In his *Confessions*, St Augustine said simply:
'His true likeness is unknown to us.'

> *Jesus, these eyes have never seen*
> *That radiant form of Thine;*
> *The veil of sense hangs dark between*
> *Thy blessed face and mine.*

> *When death these mortal eyes shall seal*
> *And still this throbbing heart,*
> *The rending veil shall Thee reveal,*
> *All-glorious as Thou art.*

'All-glorious' is the description I cherish, because it is nearest
to what Paul said, when he spoke of 'the glory of God in the
face of Jesus' (2 Corinthians 4[5]). The Gospels are impressionist
rather than photographic; but reading them, we can learn
enough. His face was a strong face—we can be sure of that.
Fishermen, and others who valued strength, followed Him.
It was a kind face—we can be sure of that—for little children
loved Him. His brow, we can be sure, was a brow unlined,
because despite all the pressing cares of life He was sure of God.
His mouth knew no cynicism or despair—though it was as

likely to break into words of denunciation where hypocrites were concerned, as to call 'Good cheer!' He was, above all, a man without sin, marked by clear courage, as when He toppled over the tables of the money-changers and drove them from His Father's House, and lashed with words the Pharisees. His eyes—whether tawny or blue—were eyes that reached to the inner secrets of the human heart, eyes that marked the simplicity of a wayside flower, the brokenhearted grief of a Peter, the time-serving choice of a Pilate.

Perhaps it is as well that we have no sure picture of Him today; it would be so easy for such to become a relic, to be fought over or worshipped.

The sublime centre of our faith is not a representation, but a Living Christ. Dr Maltby, who loved Him dearly, speaks for us all when he says: 'One may look at Jesus as He is shown to us in the Gospels for twenty years and still be overtaken by fresh wonder. . . . His heart was the home of every beatitude and a harmony of whatsoever things are true, honourable, pure, lovely and of good report. Three years of crowded toil—of unbroken peace. Preaching, teaching, healing, and all at a speed which left His companions breathless—but unhurried. He spoiled none of His gifts by haste, could wait as well as work, did nothing before the time, rose early to pray, gave nights to communion with God and found leisure to talk with a derelict woman by the well and to watch children at their play. He knew how to be alone, but He was not a recluse. The Man of Sorrows and not less the Man of Joys: serious but not strained, His humour without levity, utterly kind and utterly inexorable, tolerant and uncompromising, full of grace and truth. But no! We cannot describe Him. He is wider and greater than we know and even when we mean to praise Him, we distort the fair image of His mind and do Him wrong. Yet being what He was and is, He would not, we think, be displeased if to some of us He seems to be the most knowable Person in the world, and His human face the perfect revelation of the glory of God.'

Close To Life

ONE of my favourite poems is by my Irish friend Teresa Hooley. It appears in her *Collected Poems* which she sent me last year.

> How shall I fear to die?
>   Have I not seen
> The colour of a small blue butterfly,
>   The silver sheen
> Of breaking waves and of a wood-dove's wings?
>
> Have I not marked the coat
>   Of mouse and deer,
> The shape of flowers, the thrush's speckèd throat—
>   And shall I fear
> To fall into the Hands that made these things?

But is this argument of the heart enough—this reaching out through simple things of Nature to the Creator? The things Teresa Hooley mentions are singularly beautiful, proof of a meticulous creative care. But is it enough at death? My belief is that when I come to the great experience, I shall want more than the Creator. Jesus did—and I take my lead from Him.

Up there on the Cross, raised between earth and heaven, His last words were: 'Father . . . into Thy hands I commend My spirit.' He did not say 'Creator', but 'Father'.

I am not forgetting, of course, how greatly He loved the things of the created world—birds and flowers and winds. I think surely He must have raced as a boy up on those Nazareth hills, the wind in His hair; I know that when He was a man He talked one night about the wind that bloweth where it listeth. I know that He continually noticed the birds—simple

73

common sparrows—and the flowers growing wild by the way-side, in spring more gorgeously arrayed than Solomon. He missed nothing of the world's loveliness, and what He saw, and shared by word, became immortal.

But when He came to the great experience of death, it was not into the hands of God as Creator that He commended Himself, but into the hands of God His Father. And there is a world of difference.

One hundred and fifty times within the brief record of the Gospels that name appears. It was in His first recorded sentence, as a boy: 'Wist ye not that I must be about my Father's business?' and in His last, as a man: 'Father, into Thy hands I commend my spirit.'

Those last words of His, full of a quiet, sure trust, were, as Dr Leslie Church reminds us, 'in part a memory. He had said them as a child, in Nazareth, each night before He went to sleep. The passages a Jewish mother taught her sons were carefully chosen. Amongst them was Psalm 31. How little Mary dreamed as she repeated it over and over again to the child sitting on her knee, that one day—in a tormented hour—He would remember and cry out, "Into Thy hands I commend my spirit". But now to this fifth verse He added a word the Psalmist had not used—the word that changed a memory into an anticipation. He spoke to His Father. He was not surrendering to the pressure of inevitable circumstances, but committing Himself, with utter confidence, to God. . . . The Son was going back to His Father.'

Nature can teach us a great deal about God—God the Creator—but never enough. In Teresa Hooley's beloved Ireland there is a little church in the south, where every window but one is of painted glass. Through that single remaining clear pane, on a fine day, one may see a breath-taking view of created things—a lake of blue, studded with islets, backed by gracious hills. Most fittingly, under the window is the inscription: 'The heavens declare the glory of God, and the firmament sheweth His handiwork.' It is, of course, impressive; but it is only adequate for the worshipper who brings to it what he has already learned from Jesus of the Fatherhood of God.

So when Teresa Hooley, being Christian, sees the works of

74

the Creator's hand—the colour of a small blue butterfly, the silver sheen of breaking waves and of a wood-dove's wings, the coat of the mouse and the deer, the shape of the flowers, and the thrush's speckèd throat—she is seeing in these things more than they have to tell of God. She is impressing on their revelation of Him, as Creator, what she can only have learned from Jesus.

So when she thinks of death, she really thinks of God as *Father*, and feels safe that she falls into His hands. That is the only adequate faith; and one of the wonders of our human way is the number who have found it so. How different it is from the attitude of the sceptical Hobbes: 'I commit my body to the worms, and my spirit to the great Perhaps.' In a simple English churchyard, in the West Country, amid the quiet and beauty of trees and flowers and birds, is a Christian grave, and its stone bears but two words: 'John'—'Father'.

That is the faith of Jesus—not flashing forth in a moment, but built up through all the years. 'I thank Thee, Heavenly Father, because Thou hast hidden these things from the wise and prudent and revealed them unto babes. . . . Even so, Father, for so it seemed good in Thy sight . . . I have kept my Father's commandments and abide in His love. . . . Father, the hour is come. . . . O righteous Father, the world knew Thee not, but I know Thee. . . . Father, if Thou be willing, remove this cup from me. . . . Father, forgive them. . . . *Father, into Thy hands I commend my spirit.*'

It is into the hands of the same great Father that we commend ourselves—and those whom we love—and our world.

Through the Eyes of a Child

IN many of the places I know best, the family pew in the church is a thing of the past, and so also is family prayer in the home. There are a hundred reasons given—I know them all. But something irreplaceable is in danger. And that 'something' is religion; for it is in the home that most of us meet it first, either as a *form* or as a *force*.

Words addressed to Timothy in the first Christian century have a striking relevance in this hour, in their warning against those who 'keep up a form of religion', but 'will have nothing to do with it as a force' (2 Timothy 3⁵ Moffatt).

We make the excuse that these are difficult days for family life. They were difficult days in which Timothy was called upon to differentiate between form and force. 'For men,' say the preceding verses, 'will be selfish, fond of money, boastful, haughty, abusive, disobedient to their parents, ungrateful, irreverent, callous, relentless, scurrilous, dissolute and savage; they will hate goodness, they will be treacherous, reckless and conceited, preferring pleasure to God—for though they keep up a form of religion, they will have nothing to do with it as a force.'

This is a setting not very different from what we know today; and it is in the home, now as then, where the two standards begin to tell first. You can't deceive a child. He knows whether his parents' religion is a form or a force; he knows whether the church is to them, merely a place to go to for baptisms, marriages and funerals, and occasional festivals like Christmas and Easter, or for the very breath of their spirit, and the source of their standards for every day. You can't deceive a child. You can send him to Sunday-school and church, but if you never go yourself, he soon begins to see through it. It's very simple: religion is either a form or a force.

A charge is made against Arnold Bennett by those who shared life in the Five Towns of the potteries, that although his books made them known to the world, they gave a very poor idea of their religion. Even those with a sneaking admiration for his material success, do not find themselves easily able to forgive him that. But if he gave a derogatory impression of the Wesleyans in his Five Towns novels, it was because he wrote of what he knew. No doubt if those within his home, and those who served in the Sunday-school and church where little Enoch Arnold Bennett first met religion, had known that in their midst was an abnormally observant little boy who would one day become one of the world's great novelists, some of them would have behaved a little differently. But they didn't know; and the little boy grew up to discount their form of religion, and never knew its force. To the end of his days, his close friends said, he knew a sort of wistfulness, as he looked back to those childhood days.

How careful one needs to be when there's a child about the place. All the time he is picking up impressions that will last till the end of his life, and may well reach out to the ends of the earth.

I have been reading of the childhood of Rufus Jones, the beloved Quaker scholar and saint. There was only a bare four years between him and Arnold Bennett, yet his first contact with religion was a vastly different thing. Of his home, he wrote that 'religion there was a vital part of the air we breathed'. 'I was not "christened" in church,' he wrote, 'but I was sprinkled from morning till night with the dew of religion. We never ate a meal without a family gathering, the reading of a chapter in the Bible, followed by a period of silent worship when we talked with God, not far away, but very near.' To many moderns, such a picture of family piety suggests dourness and repression. In Rufus Jones's account of it in *A Small-Town Boy*, however, one finds about the gayest, most worthwhile story of healthy boyhood ever written. Religion in that home was no mere *form*, as Arnold Bennett found it; it was a *force*.

It is this clear distinction between form and force that marks out as an example for every true home, that home in Nazareth in which our Lord grew up. Religion was a force there.

For four hundred years there had been no prophet to break the silence, no light to dispel the darkness. Then in that obscure village 'the Rose bloomed at midnight', as the old carol puts it. Mary of Nazareth had a devout spirit; when she was greeted by her kinswoman Elizabeth, she cried out: 'My soul doth magnify the Lord.' But few makers of homes can stay for long on the devotional heights of the *Magnificat*. Ever and anon, there are meals to be made and clothes to be sewn. The carpenter's simple home was no exception. From one point of view, the saying, 'A woman's work is never done', is a commonplace; but from another it means that that work reaches up to God, and out to the ends of the earth. A woman's work is never done when it outlasts the ages. Mary's has.

In Nazareth, the boy watched how things were done—the pouring of wine into the skins, the grinding of the corn, the yeast rising in the dough, the lamps being replenished and trimmed, the baking of the bread—and from such things, long afterwards, he fashioned parables that have walked up and down in the minds of men ever since.

But Mary gave him more than a handful of everlasting stories. *'She was too near him not to perceive, even if dimly, the growth of mind and spirit within her son, and again, too wise to touch its hidden splendour, or wake before the dawn, powers meant for the day.'* When the voice of Elizabeth's son was heard crying in the wilderness, Mary knew that the hour of her own was nearly come. It came. Her young carpenter son put up the shutters at dusk for the last time. The villagers who had done business with him heard the news with surprise. The parting could no longer be stayed. On the morrow he must set his feet upon the open road, with its wider ministry, and its Cross—and his mother had to let him go.

Perhaps even yet, some artist will arise who will give us a picture of 'That Last Night in Nazareth'. But we can conjure up for ourselves a picture of that home through all the years. It was a home where religion was a force.

One feels that it must have torn His mother's heart to let Him go. Where would He sleep at night? Who would see that He got proper food? Who would mend His clothes? Perhaps He would be lonely without them all? His mother doubtless wondered all these things, as every mother in the days following the going out of the first from the home.

When He had been gone months, and came again to that little home for a night or two, what did they talk about, that Son and His mother? One feels sure they talked of God—God whom they had loved and served every day of that thirty years they had been together—God scattering the proud, putting down the mighty from their seats, filling the hungry with good things. One feels equally certain that in the days of separation which followed, Mary's thoughts turned back to what the ancient Simeon said to her in the Temple: 'Yea, a sword shall pierce thine own soul also.'

We owe Mary the mother of Nazareth a great debt. We will not worship her; we will do a far better thing—we will thank God for the ministry of her Son, our Lord, and for the high and beautiful place He has given to homes. As we look back at that home in Nazareth, 'we see the new life growing in secret', as Evelyn Underhill puts it for us. 'Nothing very startling happens. We see the child in the carpenter's workshop. He does not go outside the frame of the homely life in which He appeared. It did quite well for Him, and it will do quite well for us . . . for the pressure of God's spirit is present everywhere. Our environment itself, our home and our job, is the medium through which we experience the moulding of His besetting love.'

But when we have said what we will of Mary, we must not neglect to say something of Joseph. It takes two to make a home in which religion is a force. We know too little of Joseph; but it is illuminating to remember that when the boy, after years in that home, began to express His thoughts about God, He likened Him to a father. He would never have used and hallowed that earthly term, if Joseph had not been a good father. We have no song of his, like the *Magnificat* of Mary; but our thanks must rise to God for Mary *and* Joseph, for it needed both of them to make that home where religion was a *force* and not a *form.*

79

Today, in our homes, both 'personally and socially we are up against destructive forces'. 'Discouragement,' as Dr Fosdick reminds us, 'is a force; pessimism, fear, disillusionment, cynicism assail our souls with a power, before which only a resistant power can stand. . . . In these days of separated families and disintegrated human relationships, passion and devil-may-care recklessness of decent standards threaten even those who had thought themselves most safe.' But there is a challenge for us in this, too. 'What if in some of us a deep and conscious need should reveal for the first time that Christ, His faith about life, His way of living life, His power for sustaining life, is food for our hunger, water for our thirst, medicine for our sickness, and power to carry on—not a form but a force?'

Strangers No Longer

I STOPPED a man in the street the other day to inquire the way, and he gave me for answer: 'Sorry, I'm a stranger here myself.'

This is an age of strangers. I am not thinking especially of those who live in new building areas, where whole streets of houses seem to appear overnight, and no one can find his way—though they are typical of our time. I don't mean those people who travel with tourist over-night bags supplied by air-companies, and have constantly to ask the question I asked. I am not thinking of the Displaced Persons—that pitiful company left by war, who straggle across continents with no light in their eyes, and only a bundle of possessions on their shoulders. I am not thinking of any of these—though I can't forget them. The poet is aware of those I have in mind.

> Here lies the tragedy of our race,
> Not that men are poor—all men know something of poverty;
> Not that men are wicked—who can claim to be good?
> Not even that men are ignorant—who can boast that he is wise?
> But that men are strangers.

It is not surprising that this should be so in great cities, where thousands mill together; or even in great factories and work-shops, where workers engaged are but 'hands', or names on a pay-roll. Two recent surveys underline the fact that men and women are often strangers in these places. One of them put it plainly: 'In the cities there are innumerable rootless, restless, lonely people who are not on speaking terms either with their neighbours or with God.' Accounting for four thousand and four hundred people, employed in industry, and unhappy in their lot, the main lack was found to be not in skill or financial opportunity, but in comradeship. Deep down, they owned they were strangers, and their lot one of unhappiness and bitterness.

But this fact of our times is something that comes even closer than that—for often men and women are strangers in their own homes. The divorce court bears the most public witness, though it is not the only witness. Back in 1858 the number of divorces in England was twenty-four; and men and women who cared for the deep, rich things of life and home tried to hush it up. By 1920, it had grown to three thousand, and they couldn't hush it up. By 1944, it had grown to nineteen thousand. And today it is higher still. And every country has a similar record.

Religion, medicine and psychology, each in turn, underline the fact that without participation, co-operation, love, we die. And because this tragedy is at its centre a thing of the spirit, nothing that we can impose from the outside is of much avail. Within the home—before we move farther afield—we need to stand face to face, to be bound in one fellowship, to be rooted. This is one of the most urgent needs of our age; and without its being met, we are strangers.

Our New Zealand poet, Thomas Bracken wrote:

> *Not understood,*
> *We move along asunder,*
> *Our paths grow wider, as the seasons creep*
> *Along the years. . . .*
> *Not understood!*
> *Oh God! that men would see a little clearer,*
> *Or judge less harshly where they cannot see;*
> *Oh God! that men would draw a little nearer*
> *To one another, they'd be nearer Thee—*
> *And understood.*

But might it not be better approached from the other way? If men and women first drew nearer to God, wouldn't they find themselves nearer to each other?

Jesus was matching a deep human need when He taught us to pray, 'Our Father . . .'. For it is impossible really to pray, '*Our* Father', in a solitary state; if we use these words seriously, we are strangers no longer. When as individuals, as members of the home—not to mention the community, and the State—we say with the consent of all our faculties, 'Our Father . . .', we are soon saying: 'Our brother—Our sister—Our friend.' Upon this basis, Jesus built His Church.

'What is the Church?' asks the new Draft Catechism of the Church of Scotland? And the answer it gives is this: 'The Church is the community of those on earth and in heaven who through Jesus Christ are united in fellowship with God and with one another.' Or as one young modern put it, in an attempt to make this glorious and important truth even simpler: 'The Church is made up of those who, because they love Jesus, love God, and love one another.'

But there seem to be many people these days who do not know this great truth set at the heart of life—do not even bother to know it. 'People like my parents,' says J. B. Priestley, 'attended places of worship. Now I see that old phrase with a fresh eye. I also see how astonishing it is. Places of worship. How much have we lost, we of the younger generations, by having no places of worship? Perhaps this new world must remain desolate at heart until it achieves new places of worship.' These are striking words—words, not of a preacher, but of a modern novelist and dramatist—and life says he is right.

Jesus set His Church within reach of us all. He knew that we should always be 'desolate at heart'—strangers—unless the needs of our inmost nature were met. We are made in order that we may know God our Father, and those round about us, our brothers.

To be a stranger is life's greatest disaster.

A Favourite Chapter

BY the mercy of God, there is comfort as well as challenge in the Gospel. I was talking this week with a sister of an old people's ward in a great hospital, and she told me of one of her charges. All but blind, he requested that she would read the Bible for him each night. The last time she did this she chose that well-known chapter of John, that begins with 'Let not your heart be troubled', and goes on to speak of the Father's house of many mansions and a place prepared, and continues: 'And if I go and prepare a place for you, I will come again, and receive you unto Myself, that where I am, there ye may be also.' As she closed the Book, the old man lay down content. 'That's a nice word to go to sleep with,' he said. And it was—for he never wakened again here.

As Sister told me of it—one of the great moments of her nursing career—we went over the comfort of that great passage together. Without doubt, John 14 is one of the favourite chapters in the New Testament, especially for those who have come to the end of the way. J. M. Barrie has told us how his mother's Book always fell open at that chapter, and how when at last she was too feeble to read it, she stooped and kissed the page. It was a holy page to her—a page full of comfort for the end of the way, with its assurance of things unseen and eternal. Mary Webb has drawn us a beautiful word-picture of an old man she used to visit. She was but a child. 'On then, down the broad road between the sloping fields of miraculous green, past the roaring smithy. . . . Up three hollow steps into the dusky room, silent as one of the porches of eternity, and there was John in his Windsor chair, his black and yellow wand beside him, his great black Bible, so heavy that it made my arms ache, ready on the deal table.

84

' "Come thy ways in, my dear," he would say. "And God be with ye. A grand morning, seemingly."

' "Grand, John. And here's a snail shell in case you'd like a game of conker."

' "Nay, my dear, I be past conker. You keep it!"

' "Then I'll put it in my faery house," the child would add.

' "Ah, you do."

' "What shall I read, John?"

'He made a great show of considering, saying: "Well, there's a good few nice pieces. There's 'The greatest of these'. Then there's 'The pitcher be broken at the fountain', and 'I will give you rest'." Then he would pause, and in a moment say, as if it were a totally new idea: "How about the Many Mansions piece, my dear?" '

And the 'many mansions piece' it was.

'I had no need to look for it,' said Mary Webb, in that memory of childhood, 'the Book always fell open just there.'

The Vulgate translation 'mansiones' (from which comes our Authorized Version 'mansions') is used of resting-places on a road. They are really caravanserais—shelters at stages along the road where travellers may rest on their journey. In the East this pleasant arrangement has long obtained—and does still, where modern transport has not penetrated. And it was the custom for travellers to send a dragoman on ahead of them, to make preparations for their coming at the next resting-place. It is thought that our Lord had this in mind when He presented Himself as our spirit's dragoman. It is a word full of comfort. 'Quite frankly,' says Dr George MacLeod, 'the idea of "mansions in heaven" conveyed little to my mind till I came across the researches of another, who pointed out that the word mansions does not exclusively mean houses, but is the old English translation of the Latin word "mansiones". . . . Some of you old campaigners, soldiers and nurses, will remember when battalions had to go long distances (especially in the East) on well-defined routes, every fifteen miles or so there were recognized villages with billets there, or rest-houses. Do you remember, as the battalion moved along, how almost always the quarter-master rode ahead to prepare billets, and so often used to ride back to meet us and guide us for the last mile home?

'Or if war is not your recollection, you will find in travel-books of the East constant references to travellers crossing the desert with guides, the novice traveller getting in a panic half-way through the day to find the guide has disappeared from the party, only to discover later that he has really gone ahead to arrange billets for the night, and comes again at evening to meet the party coming in.

'Looked at this way, the whole text leaps to life,' says Dr MacLeod.

This favourite passage for old folk is seen to hold much more than comfort for the end of the day. It has a message for us all as we struggle along. No part of the journey is unfamiliar to our Lord—if there are times when we seem to be forsaken, we have only to remember that He has gone on a little ahead to prepare the next resting-place.

Ringing Words

TO listen to a powerful and persuasive speaker is a pleasure all too rare. Cosmo Lang tells of a prisoner whom he met during his incumbency at Portsea, in the course of his duties at the local prison. He had been reading his Bible. Lang asked him what he thought of the particular prophet whose words he'd been reading. His reply was: 'I'd like to 'ave 'eard that chap on the Town 'all steps!'

When I read Paul's defence before Agrippa I feel the same. Even after this interval of time his words, I find, are irresistible. What must it have been like to have heard him, against the colour and pageantry of that historic occasion!

Strictly, of course, the setting was not a trial, but something near to an entertainment. Festus has succeeded Felix as Governor of Judea. He is a figure of considerable authority. And Herod comes to pay his respects to the new governor. To grace the official visit, he brings with him his sister Bernice, a young woman in her late teens, in the bloom of her beauty.

As a matter of interest, Festus mentions the prisoner he happens to hold in custody at the moment. Perhaps Agrippa would like to hear the man in the morning; it might prove a pleasant diversion. And Agrippa agrees.

In the morning, Paul is led before them—in one of the State rooms of the palace. In royal purple, accompanied by his queen and her ladies in silks and jewels, the Governor in scarlet, and his escort of officers, Agrippa hears Paul.

True, his defence begins with disarming courtesy: 'I think myself happy, King Agrippa, because I shall answer for myself this day before thee touching all the things whereof I am accused of thee among the Jews: wherefore I beseech thee to hear me patiently.' But soon he is recounting the most amazing story of all time—ending with an empty tomb, and a Risen Lord. Like all men whose lives are revolutionized by some decisive event, Paul has a ringing sincerity, and his speech has a kind of grandeur about it that befits the occasion. He marshals his facts with skill, and presents them with undeniable power. Paul, who appears small as he begins to speak, seems no longer small. As he recounts his own striking experience of the Risen Christ, the shining truth is lighted with eloquence. And how he runs it home—'This thing was not done in a corner' (Acts 26[26]).

Here lies the truth of the matter. And those who listen to him, know it. The events of Bethlehem might, as it were, have been done in a corner. The birth of a baby, when people were busy about other matters, could easily pass unnoticed. Much the same might be admitted of Nazareth—a little village, off the beaten ways of the world, with a somewhat doubtful reputation. But not this—this greatest event of all, the death and resurrection of Jesus. This happened in Jerusalem, and at the Feast time when thousands surged through the city streets; and beside a great Roman roadway. A cross dropped into its socket amid soldiers and a crowd was a public spectacle. That was what it was intended to be; it was like the hangings at Tyburn which took place in the England of crueller days—at the junction of the main roads—the most populous place that could be found. The crucifixion of Jesus did not take place in a corner. Nor did the more amazing happening, the Resurrection. And in that morning light, Paul the little aristocrat—made over again by that mighty happening—drives it home.

True, Agrippa might argue 'perhaps, after all, Jesus did not really die: could He not have just swooned, and been taken down from the Cross, to revive later in the coolness of the rock-lined tomb?' But no, Pilate had provided against such a happening by ordering His side to be pierced. Had He but swooned, when he revived He must have shown signs of being desperately wounded by that sword-thrust, and He could hardly have impressed anyone with having triumphed over death. No, that would not do.

There was, of course, another possibility. The earliest news of His having risen had been brought to His disciples by a

88

woman. She had lived through days and nights of strain—and was in need of sleep. Agrippa might have argued that being nervously overwrought, in the dim light of the dawn, she had *imagined* she saw Him. But even whilst he entertained the thought, the proud listener would have been obliged to dismiss it. For hallucinations, he would know, do not readily occur unless the event be eagerly expected and longed for. And nothing was farther from the minds of those whom Jesus had gathered round Him as disciples. One of them, Thomas, had even refused to believe the resurrection on the witness of several of his most trusted friends. And there was another difficulty—the theory hardly accounted for the way in which the story had spread, until hundreds of otherwise ordinary, normal people were as certain that He was risen as those who first told the story. And there was the major difficulty of explaining how the tomb came to be empty. At the time, the authorities had been at a loss to do anything about it—in the whole crowded city, they had not found a single witness who could refute the empty tomb. If there had been such a person, certainly he had not come forward. What was even more awkward, those who made the claim— His very mixed band of disciples, cast down into the depths by the events of His death—were suddenly transformed. That was perhaps the hardest thing of all to explain away, added to the fact that they had begun to tell their story, not after an interval of time when men had forgotten the details, or in some distant part where not much had been heard about it, but in the very city where it had happened, and at once.

Paul's ringing words underlined these strange facts. In very truth, 'this thing was not done in a corner!'

The resurrection is a fact, and to acknowledge it, as Archbishop Temple said so confidently and so clearly, 'is to share in a new movement of life, and to co-operate with new regenerating forces which have entered history'. The fact of the Risen Christ is vastly more than a remarkable story, beloved of the Church, and told again Easter by Easter. If we would have the witness of a historian, let it be our contemporary, Professor Arnold Toynbee. He closes the sixth volume of his monumental survey of the rise and fall of nations with a confidence like

Paul's, as he stood that morning before Agrippa. Discussing the various 'saviours' of mankind, who by philosophy or sword have presented their claims and passed away, he says, in the end 'our motley host has dwindled to a company of none but gods. At the final ordeal of death, few, even of these saviour-gods had dared to put their title to the test by plunging into the icy river. And now as we stand and gaze with our eyes fixed on the farther shore a single Figure rises and straightway fills the whole horizon. There is the Saviour, "and the pleasure of the Lord shall prosper in His hand and He shall see of the travail of His soul and shall be satisfied".'

Yes, 'this thing was not done in a corner'—and we shall fail to grasp the significance of life, for the world, and for ourselves, if we push the Lord of this mighty happening into a corner. I was walking one of the mean streets of London, one afternoon, when of a sudden I came on a branch of the Methodist London Mission. Bombs had fallen, and part of the place was in ruins —tidied up as best ruins could be, but ruins still. Near by, on that mean street, the missioner, with faith and insight, had taken a shop-front; and as I looked at it, I found it had been transformed into a 'Street Sanctuary'—a place of beauty and significance for the passer-by—a rather plain communion-table, and upon it a wooden cross and a vase of flowers. Behind, on the wall, hung three pictures, and on a low wooden stand was an open Bible. As I paused beside a silent workman who had removed his cloth cap to read, that mean, ruined street was transformed: for the words on the open page were: 'Now is Christ risen from the dead.' That was a fact to be reckoned with there in Bermondsey!

> *After three days! And even as He said,*
> *Lo, with the rising morn He rose again.*
> *After three days—and with Him from the dead,*
> *Hope rose immortal, in the hearts of men.*

Neville Talbot served as a soldier; he was President of the Oxford Union, Chaplain of Balliol College, and Bishop of Pretoria, but he will be longest remembered as the force behind Talbot House. A giant of a man, both physically and spiritually, he had glorious energies, and men loved him. He married lovely Cecil Mary Eastwood. And suddenly, with the birth of their second child, she died. But in that dark hour, Talbot was able to rise in his grief and cable home: 'Darling Cecil died. . . . Baby well. Christ is risen!'

It is a fact to be reckoned with in life's most real experience—a fact not to be pushed into any corner.

Happy Pilgrims

THE years have a way of dimming the sharp edges of experience, but I shall always be glad that on my first visit to England, I walked with pack on back down the old Pilgrim's Way, to 'Canterbury-towne'. Ever since, the very word 'pilgrim' has been a shining word to me: an unhappy pilgrim a contradiction in terms. Chaucer's *Canterbury Tales*, I must confess—till Nevill Coghill gave us his translation over the BBC, and more recently in the Penguin Classics—seemed a little difficult; but there has never been any doubt about the happiness that attended that pilgrimage. An old manuscript penned shortly after Chaucer's death underlines the same happiness. 'I say to thee,' it begins, 'that it is well done that Pilgrims have with them singers and also pipers, and that when one of them that goeth bare-foot, striketh his toe upon a stone, and hurteth it sore, and maketh him to bleed, it is well done that he or his fellow begin then a song, or else take out of his bosom a pipe to drive away with such mirth the hurt of his fellow.' It was of the very nature of their pilgrimage that they should know the happiness of a good purpose, in good company, to a good end.

And Dr Moffatt has nothing less in mind when he translates Psalm 84[5]: 'Happy are they who, nerved by Thee, set out on pilgrimage.'

It is a pity that so many of us nowadays have dropped the idea of the spiritual life being a pilgrimage. Dr Leslie Church says: 'We cease to be tramps and become pilgrims, when we decide on a goal. We go on from stage to stage, each one nearer our "Canterbury". We can't be pilgrims to Nowhere.'

In dropping the term, perhaps, we confirm a judgement often

made against us, that *we lack a strong sense of direction*, and also a second charge, that *we are not characterized by 'pilgrim happiness'*.

This is not to overlook the fact that things both puzzling and painful quite often happen to the pilgrim. As the old manuscript says, he may well stub his toe, and make it to bleed sore. There is no guarantee that he will be immune from the common disasters that meet others upon the way; far from it. Then he must take out of his bosom the hidden consolations of his faith, like a little reed pipe on which to make music, or he must summon up from the secret places of his own being the song that his God has taught him to sing.

The inference of Scripture is that he will almost certainly meet with difficulties of some kind. At the very outset, he is warned to consider well the hazards of the way.

But despite anything that can happen, the glorious happiness of the pilgrim is assured. The Psalmist is right: 'Happy are they who, nerved by Thee, set out on pilgrimage.' The secret lies in the fact that his happiness is not at the mercy of things that can happen. In youth, he may set out hopefully, the good green earth beneath his feet, the blue sky overhead. But it is too much to hope that his religious pilgrimage will always be of that kind. At some stage his feelings of youthful eagerness are bound to desert him; the way will lead uphill, over uneven places; at times he may even doubt whether the whole undertaking is worth his effort. He may have real difficulty in picking out the way.

Wilfred Pickles tells of an hour he spent with an old fisherman of Kirkcudbright. Asked about the way he had come, he answered: ' "That's a tall order, but I'll gie ye a wee keek into my life." Then, with a far-away look in his deep blue eyes, he recalled some of the fellows he had known.' They were not unfamiliar with the 'stubbed toe' of the way; they had travelled with dull skies overhead; but that was not the most important thing about them, and their going. There was a light in the old fisherman's eyes, as one by one he called them to mind. ' "And then," said he, "there was auld Andy. Puir auld Andy some people would call him. I can see him now going down the street after digging for lugworms for bait, wi' his can on his back, and his hair streaming on his shoulders, an' singin', as only his could sing,

> 'Ah'm a pilgrim bound for glory;
> Ah'm a pilgrim coming home!' " '

As we journey with a distant light in our eyes, we are not totally unmindful of the Here and Now—far from it. For we do not travel alone; a solitary pilgrim is an impossibility, in the life of the spirit. Always there is some fellow to help, some situation to improve for those who follow, some piece of truth to learn and to carry with us.

The real danger is not lest our eyes should be on the Hereafter —a charge often made—but lest loving this world with all its human delights, we should settle down Here and Now, and forget that we are pilgrims.

The Living Vine

BEFORE me in well-filled pews this morning were house-wives, mothers, and retired business-women. I had been called to talk about 'The Vine'. It was good to be there—and yet in some ways, it was a pity. I had much rather we had spent our Friday morning out-of-doors, preferably up on a Henderson hillside.

Jesus suffered neither handicap that I knew—His people were not lifted out of their normal setting; and His text was not lifted out of a Holy Book, written in another age, another tongue, another land. He spoke of the things that made up daily life—the housewife making her bread; the mother putting a patch on a worn garment; the sower, going up and down his precious little piece of soil, casting his seed right and left; the anxious shepherd, seeking his sheep. And the people understood. So they did when He talked about the Vine; it was as much part of their life as the breath they breathed, the sky over their heads, the earth under their feet.

We are not daily concerned with the care and talk of vines; we do not live in the midst of them. Yet we do live in the midst of the ageless truth that Jesus used them to convey.

To overcome our difficulty as best I could, I spent some part of an afternoon lately with an old man up on a Henderson hillside. His whole life is given to vines; and at this time of the year—the season of fruitfulness—he is out with them from five in the morning till darkness falls. His people in Yugoslavia have tended vines for two hundred years. So vines, and talk of vines are very close to him.

It was just as easy and as natural for Jesus to talk to His disciples that night, about the vine and the branches, the pruning and the fruit. They had just broken bread together in the Upper Room, and shared the cup—with its juice of the crushed grape. At that moment, as they left the house in the light of the Paschal moon, a grape-vine likely trailed along a wall in the garden, or the pungent smell of the smouldering fires of the vine-dressers, who were burning their prunings in the valley below, rose up to meet their quickened senses in the night air.

In many a Palestinian family, there was no livelihood apart from the care of their terraced vine-yard. A good deal of the land was poor and much of it was stony, but the climate suited the growing of vines, which reached luscious fruitfulness during the prolonged sunshine and the dewy nights of late summer. From time beyond memory the vine with its clusters had provided their fruit supply, dried raisins for trade, and thirst-quenching drink.

Thus, to Jesus and to His listeners, the vine was a familiar sight and a familiar idea. Their day-to-day knowledge was further strengthened by the fact that from infancy they had been brought up on the Old Testament prophets, where the vine was a commonplace. They could not forget Isaiah's word-picture of the vine-grower setting about his task, selecting a fruitful hill, digging it, planting it, protecting it.

Nor did they miss the prophet's reference to Jesus Himself, as the shoot out of the stock of Jesse: 'And there shall come forth a rod out of the stem of Jesse, and a branch out of his roots shall bear fruit.' And all through Christ's ministry, they had become familiar with His use of the vine to underline the relevance of His teaching. They had heard Him speak of the labourers in the vineyard; they remembered His word about the two sons —the one who promised to go and work in his father's vineyard and went not, and the other who made no promises but went; they never forgot His story about the owner who found himself with more than he could manage, and let out his vineyard to others; they heard Him tell of the mistaken effort of the thrifty who put new wine into old skins—and left somebody to clean up the mess and lament the waste; and there was that occasion when He asked—surely with a little smile playing about His lips—'Do men gather grapes of thorns, or figs of thistles?'

As they stepped from the Upper Room that night, they did not miss His point when He spoke of Himself as the Vine. And it was a wonderful thing that He told them.

First, there was the emphasis on His *one-ness* with those to whom He spoke. 'I am the Vine,' said He; 'ye are the branches.' And the message that He spoke that night to those first disciples, He speaks as surely to us. Where could He have found a better picture of one-ness? We may well marvel at its aptness:

> *The living Vine. Christ chose it for Himself—*
> *He did not choose the summer corn,*
> *That shoots up straight and free in one quick growth. . . .*
> *But only this for Him and His in one—*
> *The everlasting, ever-quickening Vine.*

What is the vine without the branches? You must let me bring life and beauty to you, He says in effect; it must happen as naturally as the vital sap rises in the vine. We are made for each other. 'Apart from Me ye can do nothing.'

But do we understand it?—in our personal religious life? in our Church life? We live amid rush and tear, and feverish organized effort. 'Without Me ye can do nothing,' says Jesus. Why have we so often failed? We have forgotten the one-ness between the vine and the branches; we have acted as if we could bear fruit of ourselves—with a little more effort. So when our life has appeared fruitless, we have bustled around and set up another committee. 'A committee,' someone has said, 'is a group of people who individually can do nothing, but collectively are able to decide that nothing can be done.' That may not be strictly true—we must make room for a twinkle in the eye—but this is true, on the authority of Jesus: 'Without Me ye can do nothing.'

And yet, if we could only grasp it, this one-ness is just what we need. See how it lifts the responsibility. We are only branches—we are not responsible for the fruit—we are not the source of that vital life-giving sap that rises to transform everything. The branches bear fruit simply by their one-ness with the vine. It doesn't depend on the branches; it depends on the vine. It doesn't depend on us; it depends on Him.

Every virtue we possess,
And every victory won,
And every thought of holiness
Are His alone.

A young artist complained to Blake that life had gone out of his work, that inspiration had ceased. Blake listened, then turned to his wife, and said simply: 'It is so with us, sometimes, is it not, for weeks together. What do we do then?' And his wife said: 'We kneel down and pray.' In other words, we do something to restore the one-ness out of which all true life comes. This is the first truth that Jesus wants us to grasp.

And the second is as relevant. Jesus draws attention to the discipline of the pruning-knife. The face of the old vine-grower with whom I talked up on his sunny hillside clouded as I spoke of it. 'This,' said he, lowering his tone a little, 'this is an operation that wrings the heart at first. All that lovely green growth cut away! It's hard to learn what it means. Unless you prune hard you will not get your crop.' And he led me from vine to vine to emphasize his meaning. 'You see this one,' he said, 'you see all this growth, all these leaves—I must cut it all back. It is a hard lesson to learn.'

And in the things of the spirit it is no less so. 'Discipline,' says the writer to the Hebrews, 'always seems for the time to be a thing of pain, not of joy: but those who are trained by it reap the fruit of it afterwards' (Hebrews 12[11], Moffatt).

Of course, it is the '*afterwards*' that matters. There is only one purpose in this one-ness, this pruning: Fruit! Fruit! Fruit!

We know what the fruits of the Spirit are—and set down in Moffatt's translation, they are just what we most want: love, joy, peace, good temper, kindliness, generosity, fidelity, gentleness, self-control—real day-to-day qualities. Evelyn Underhill sums it all up for us in *The Fruits of The Spirit*: 'The spiritual life consists in His action within us. . . . His sap rising quietly and secretly in the soul, bringing forth, not merely nice devotional flowers—but fruits.'

Sure Hands

IN life's great moments there is no escaping a sense of inadequacy. The Psalmist knew it. And he stayed himself on the greatness of God. 'The Lord is a great God,' he cried, 'and a great King above all gods. In His hands are the deep places of the earth: the strength of the hills is His also. The sea is His, and He made it: and His hands formed the dry land. O come, let us worship and bow down, let us kneel before the Lord our Maker!'

Men spoke much then about the hands of God, fashioning and leading and redeeming. 'My times are in Thy hands', was the strength of their relationship. And when their earthly pilgrimage was at an end, they thought of themselves nowhere so secure as in the hands of God.

There is something timeless in that. We have grown more skilful—we have explored the deep places of the earth, bringing forth its treasures to serve our needs and our whims—gold, coal, tin, and now uranium to help make the atom bomb that brings terror to our hearts. We have climbed the hills, with our sticks and our own stubborn energies; we have climbed and mastered the mountains, even the mightiest of them, Everest. The sea has been made to surrender its sands, its pearls, its sponges, and to provide food for our tables. The dry land has been discovered, claimed, mapped—and fought over, till the passion for its possession has cursed us all with bloodshed.

But our skills are not enough we find; always life drives us back to the same shattering sense of our own inadequacy that the Psalmist knew. Life is too big for us; and death is too big.

Who can forget that moment in our time when a man stood silhouetted sharp in the moonlight, on the crest of a little hill, looking out to sea? In front of him spread a glittering waste of waters. Near by stood a little handful of officers, men like himself. And together they watched big ships, little ships, grey monsters of the deep, destroyers, tankers, freighters, full of men. Overhead planes circled and zoomed. Only in the heart of that man who looked down on that assemblage of mechanized might as its leader, was there silence—the silence of inadequacy. They saw him draw himself up to attention, and lift his hand to the salute. Then they saw him drop his hand, and his head—and the silent moments passed. They knew what he was doing: he was praying, for he was that kind of man. That great human armada was setting out for Sicily, and he commanding it.

When he spoke again, those nearest to him never forgot his words: 'There comes a time when you have done all that you can possibly do; when you have used your brains, your training, your technical skill, and the die is cast, and events are in the hands of God—and there you have to leave them.' That man was General Eisenhower, in his strength, and in his inadequacy.

Life does that to us—to even the strongest of us, the most technically skilful, the most financially proud. The moment comes when we are only secure if we know ourselves in the hands of God.

And what we discover, at great cost, as a nation, life forces us to know, at some time or other, as individuals. There comes a grave illness, an operation, a moment of sharp decision, an added responsibility—and who is sufficient? Anne Sedgwick, the novelist, at seventy, puts it like this: 'Life is a queer struggle, but life is beautiful to me. There is joy in knowing that I lie in the hands of God.'

With that faith, life is never too big for us. One of the most memorable glimpses of that great woman Daisy Bates, the friend of the aborigines, was in the way she taught them to think of death. For nearly forty years she loved them and followed them from place to place in her white tent, losing herself, it seemed to some, in that great continent with its rim of cities and a dying race at its heart. She dealt with cannibal-practices and tribal warfare, the only woman on whom they ever conferred blood-brotherhood. They called her *Kabbarli*, grandmother. She became a legend in her own time; the King gave her the O.B.E., but the honour she valued most was that of being *Kabbarli* to her own children of the scattered tribes. She collected her water-supply from a creek, and her mail from any handy post-top. I travelled hundreds of miles in that hot, merciless continent with a stockman who sometimes carried *Kabbarli's* mail.

When her children of the great spaces reached out beyond life to death, she told them of God the Father. 'To one by one,' said she, 'when that moment comes, I put out my hand, and holding the departing child of the bush, I say, "I will hold you safely by the hand, and when you have to let go, God will take hold of your other hand".'

One Family

'TOGETHERNESS' has not yet found its way into our dictionary, though it is a good, rich word, close to life. Many of us have yet to accept what Edward Rogers calls 'Paul's shrewd comment that "we are members one of another". Not,' he continues, 'that we ought to be, but that we are.' 'We are in one terrestial household whether we like it or not, and there is nowhere to move to, this side of Jordan—at least,' he adds with a twinkle, 'until the inter-planetary service is operating.' That is still rather remote, even if there were any certainty that the Creator of our world has created those un-visited planets to observe a different law. Here, at any rate, 'we are members one of another'—and in this age of world-shrinkage which is the outcome of our modern feats of transport and communication, it has become a problem of far-reaching consequences. 'It is easy,' Edward Rogers adds, 'to get on well with your relations if you never meet them; but when you and your wife and family and mother-in-law and Uncle Joe and Aunt Lucy and their children and Grandma's second cousin are all living together, you can expect trouble about the use of the bathroom and the cooker and the best armchair—unless you are a disciplined and loving family. The analogy,' he says, 'is exact, and the conclusion inescapable.'

Paul uses the words, 'we are members one of another', to underline this God-given law as it operates in the Church. But the same law runs through all life—geographic, economic, domestic. This is the kind of world God has made, and the kind of people He has made us. 'This,' says Dr H. H. Farmer, 'is the ulti-mate secret of finite personal nature, of specifically human nature. Only as man is part of, held in, that structure, is he distinctively man. If, *per impossible*, you could lift a man out of it, he would cease to exist as man. It is not that God creates a man and then pops him into a world of persons as a housewife makes a dumpling and pops it into the saucepan, both dumpling and saucepan being capable of existing apart from one another. To come into existence as a man,' he sums up, 'is to be incorporated in this world of the personal, to be in relation to persons—the divine person and human persons—and existence as a man is not possible on any other terms.' Both Rogers and Farmer are prepared to forsake their stately theological terms for the moment, in order that even the most domesticated of us may grasp this fundamental law. For it is so important. We can't hope to make much of life unless we recognize it.

From the very fact that 'we are members one of another' comes, in the first place, so much that enriches our life, so much 'unearned happiness'. It is good to remember this when we are tempted to bewail the 'undeserved suffering' that comes to us. Both are inescapable, and it is well to recognize them—the law and the counter-law of all our human experience.

We come into life here, rich in many things because 'we are members one of another'. Centuries of medical skill and mothersense, go into our very reception. We each inherit the safety and love of a home prepared, without which entry into this strangely complex life would be an altogether hazardous undertaking. On the mental plane, the whole of literature is here waiting for us—though at first we are satisfied with nurseryrhymes and with rag-books. When we are ready, the school as generously awaits us, leading on to the college and university. No less, on the highest plane, the spiritual, 'we are members one of another'. We are received as infant members of the Church, and as we grow through the kindergarten, the Sunday-school class, the youth camp and training-group, we enter into the rich happiness of Christian living. All the accumulated devotional life of the ages is as surely ours—all the hymns that other hearts have fashioned out of experience, now put together in our hymn-books; all the great prayers set together in devotional manuals; all the glorious self-sacrificing missionary effort of the Church. And there is music and art, each a rich heritage that could never be ours save for this gracious law, not to mention the many practical public services that we thankfully receive, and daily use. No one but an All-wise Creator could have made such a wonderful world and set us in it.

On the other side, of course, is the counter-law of 'undeserved suffering'. And this is where trouble starts for most of us; and it will always remain, until we see these two areas of experience springing out of the same law, that 'we are members one of another'. If we are ready to benefit from the 'unearned happiness', then we must be prepared to bear the 'undeserved suffering'. That seems fair, and it is a fact that we must take into account in our day to day living. It is no use saying, when suffering comes as the result of others' ignorance or foolishness: 'It isn't fair, why should this happen to me?' There is no escape; this is the way life is made. We cannot extricate ourselves from this all-wise pattern; and is there any reason why we should? 'We are members one of another.'

A Birthday

ARE you good at remembering birthdays? It's quite a task, even within the family. Beyond the family, it becomes almost impossible—unless one has a birthday-book, a good memory, or both.

The family of our young princess H.R.H. Alexandra is saved that trouble. Her birthday is on the 25th December. It seems impossible that they could forget that date. I remember when she was born. King George the Fifth had just died, and a widespread sadness lay over the royal family, and the kingdom. And then was born this little Princess—on the 25th December.

Years have sped, and now she is almost through her teens—developing into a beautiful and poised young person. If you should be walking in the little Buckingham village of Iver, as I have done, you might meet her—a tall young girl in tweed skirt and bright sweater, taking her dog for an outing. Or you might see her, as simply clad, riding through the wooded lanes. Or you might happen upon her shopping—for shopping has always been fun to her, since with her young schoolboy brother, she spent her Saturday sixpence. 'Coppins', her country home, has come to be known—in name, at least—all over the world. And our thoughts will turn there once again this year, on the 25th December—for it is the birthday of a Princess.

But our thoughts will turn even more surely to another simple setting, to keep the birthday of the young Prince, the Prince of Peace. We have no possible excuse for forgetting that date—the same 25th December—though we may need forgiveness for thinking it just a holiday, when it is something much more.

> *Still Bethlehem the town*
> *Lies where it lay long years ago,*

Still brown-faced children play
Through crooked streets
And wander on the hills,
Still men sow seed and harvest grain,
Still women bake.

But all the world
Goes the more bravely to its task
Because once, long ago,
A little child was born
In Bethlehem.

Christmas is, above all, a Birthday. It is a happiness to have time off from work—and the more taxing the year, the more welcome this respite. But that is not all; and we go back to our work little changed when the goodwill has worn off, and the tinsel and wrapping-papers are put away, unless we celebrate much more on the 25th December. A holiday isn't enough for our human hearts—we need a Birthday. And God has given us a Birthday!

I shall never forget putting a number of little boys to bed at a Christmas Camp. As I heard them say their prayers, finishing with the Lord's Prayer: 'forgive us our trespasses', one little fellow prayed: 'forgive us our Christmases'. It is a prayer that many of us could pray. I do not say that we should not have colour and festivity at Christmas—we have the greatest reason in the world for having them—but all these things ought surely to be the outward expression of the central fact, not a substitute for it.

The heart of Christmas is that once in history God, the Eternal, the Creator of the heavens and the earth, stepped down into human life, with all its sin and sorrow and noisy clamour; that He came a little Child, at the end of nine months of womanly patience; that He walked this human way, meeting life where men and women worked and worshipped and wrangled; that, determined to be rid of Him, they raised a tall beam, with another roughly hammered to it to make a cross, and upon that cross crucified Him. It is an incredible story. Yet it's the story

Rita F. Snowden

PRINCE AND DARLING—FAITHFUL WORKERS

that ties heaven and earth together on the 25th December. It's not a pretty story, much less a pretty-pretty one, dependent on tinsel and trappings, fit only to be told to small children and the starry-eyed. Far from it. It is the strongest, most transforming fact in the whole world. The very absence of what we might call a 'Christmassy' setting but serves to emphasize what Dr Whale expresses so well: 'The Son of God came into history, He did not come out of it.'

One has only to think of the setting. Rome, the great military power, enjoyed world-dominion; only a comparative minority nursed in their hearts a living faith; to the lot of the favoured, Greece added her contribution of culture, but for the great mass of common people—slaves many of them—life was hard. There were no jaunty robins on sprigs of holly, no high-wheeled coaches unloading travellers before a lighted inn, no little pointed firs weighted down with snow, no Christmas cards—it wasn't like that. But that first Birthday was something so real that it reached right down to the bottom-most need of the human heart. The centre of it wasn't even children, but One Child, the Holy Child Jesus, and a call to worship God in what was revealed in Him.

And that remains the heart of Christmas. If it were not as real as that, it would be hardly worth talking about in the kind of world we have today.

But God still waits, in power and in love, that we may even yet receive into our hearts, into our national and international life, not a holiday, but a Birthday! That is what Christmas means. To sum it up simply: 'The Eternal God enters our common life with all the energy of His creative love ... speaking our language, and showing us his secret beauty on our own scale.' A Birthday! It may yet be for us, and for our world, the beginning of a new life—that is what a Birthday means.

The High Ways of Humility

THE tables in the café where I sometimes take a cup of coffee are so close together that it is impossible not to overhear snatches of conversation. It is a happy place and is almost always pleasantly full. This morning, as I lingered over my coffee before setting off into the crisp sunshine, a word lodged in my mind, and I couldn't get rid of it. A couple were in conversation. She said to him: 'It shouldn't have been allowed to happen. You know, I was *humbled* to the ground.'

Off and on during the business of the day, I found myself thinking about that word. Perhaps what she meant was 'humiliated' rather than 'humbled'—for humiliations are from without, humility is from within. St Bernard's saying seemed suddenly to come alive: 'We are all humiliated, but we are not all humble.'

Of course, the word 'humble' is not very well understood these days—it has lost much of its dignity, and has taken on a Uriah Heepish condescension. The latin *humilitas* means a debased, cowardly condition. But the word humility, as it is employed in Christian usage, has a different content—it is much less what we bear, than what we are. It in no way smacks of the cringing of Uriah Heep.

Dr Truman Douglass had a twinkle in his eye when he spoke of the Carmelite who compared his Order with others. 'Of course,' said he, 'for scholarship, we cannot compare with the Benedictines; and for charity we cannot match the good works of the Franciscans; but in humility, we are superior to everyone on the earth.' Humility so loudly aware of itself is certainly not humility.

Humility is rather a lovely upstanding quality, the sign of a big nature. 'The true way to be humble,' Phillips Brooks used to say, 'is not to stoop until you are smaller than yourself, but to stand at your real height against some higher nature.' I like that. I have seen humility both in the Scriptures and in daily life. Peter came to it that way; Peter had little idea of humility till he stood to his full height, day after day, in the presence of his Risen Lord. Then it seemed to him a quality of such importance that he wrote to his friends a most surprising thing—for Peter: 'Be clothed in humility' (1 Peter 5⁵).

Dr Albert Schweitzer is still, in his snowy-headed eighties, in the primeval forest at Lambarene. Lately two visitors from the noisy outside world called on him in his hospital, and that memorable visit was reported in the *Manchester Guardian*. It was ten years since he had consented to a formal interview. His visitors found him a vigorous man, still able to work from six in the morning till after midnight, and engaged, in addition to his hospital work, on writing the third volume of his *Philosophy of Civilization*. Tucked away in his modest study-bedroom, they saw stacks of completed manuscript, for which the world would give much. Some of the chapters, he confessed, had been re-written six times. As each chapter was finished, he looped it with a string, and with a smile, hung it modestly on a nail, 'just,' he confessed, 'as a hunter would hang a pheasant.' The idea seemed to be that even his best work needed time to mature.

When his two admirers took their leave of him, it was noticed that beside their names in the visitors' book they had inscribed a description of him: 'Greatest Soul in Christendom.' When the Doctor chanced upon it, those present scarcely remembered seeing him more distressed. 'No, no, never,' said he; and as he rose from expunging the offending tribute, it seemed to them that he stood to his full height in the presence of his Risen Lord.

No one can charge Albert Schweitzer with cringing—before men and women, before herculean tasks, or before truth—but standing in the presence of his Lord, he knows full well the measure of humility.

We may puzzle over a word as we go about our business; we may pause too seldom to read what Peter wrote; but God, in His mercy, does not leave us without a witness, lest we miss our way.

Crowds

DO you like crowds? Do you sometimes enjoy being in the streets when the shops and factories come out, and people are hurrying home to their evening meal? I do. It is individuals that one picks out at first, this one with the funny hat, that one with the stick and a limp. Then there are the mouths—the mouths that go up at the corners and look rather jolly, the mouths that go down at the corners and look rather grumpy. And there is the variety of the women's coats and frocks—some of them smart, some of them dowdy, some of them, one suspects, not yet paid for; and the men's suits—some of them smartly pressed, a few of them dull and worn, an odd one or two ill-fitting. Together, men and women, they make up the crowd—all intent, all surging somewhere. And one is liable to feel a little overwhelmed.

London crowds are specially liable to make one feel like that: they are so great. A nurse friend told me of her experience. For a while the crowds milling along fascinated her, but after a short time they became too much. People—men and women, all unknown to her, tall, short, fat, thin, rich, poor, and all milling along.

One evening she decided to go for a walk in one of the parks. Then, realizing that it was dusk, she as suddenly remembered what her relations had told her. So she stepped out of her way a little to where a policeman, a reassuring tower of blue, stood directing the traffic. 'Is it all right,' she asked, 'to walk alone in the park at this time of the day?'

Still mechanically waving his arms to urge on the traffic, he looked her up and down: 'Where do you come from?' he asked. 'You come from Australia?'

'No, I don't,' she answered, and made to walk off.

'Ah, you come from New Zealand,' he called after her. 'Look, I used to walk out with a girl from Wanganui.' (One of our towns, down in the country. Only he called it *Wang-er-nui*.)

At that, my friend turned on her heels, and came back, her face all aglow. 'Did you really?' she asked. 'Now, isn't that wonderful!'

It was wonderful. London, in that moment, was not just a city of swirling crowds. Here was an individual, and she was still an individual—neither was completely lost in the crowd. That's an important discovery when one is 12,000 miles from home. It's an important discovery any time, anywhere.

Life today is becoming more and more impersonal; industry a matter of larger and larger combines. Mass production with its regimentation is the setting in which millions must earn their living before they pour out into the streets. There was a time when each worker was known as an individual, but that has now largely gone—swallowed up in the vast impersonal terms, 'capital', 'labour', 'personnel'. Never were human beings so jostled, never was life so turbulent, so crowded.

But for all that, crowds have a striking way of breaking up into individuals—life is made like that. 'The streets are alive with people,' as Wells said, 'grave, decorous-looking people. They pass intent upon their various businesses with the air of knowing exactly what they are doing.' But then he goes on to pick out one and another who belies that impression—the girl who is all but frantic over a choice she has to make; a gentleman, debonair on the streets, who stares out of his window with the dawn, and wishes, and comes near to contriving, another man dead.

One of the most striking word-pictures in the Gospels shows us exactly the same thing—the crowd, surging and jostling, presently breaking up to reveal the individual. You remember it? (Luke 8: Moffatt's rendering) 'As Jesus went, the crowds kept crushing Him, and a woman who had a haemorrhage for twelve years, which no one could cure, came up behind Him and touched the tassel of His robe. Her haemorrhage instantly ceased: Jesus said, "Who touched Me?" As everyone denied it,

III

Peter and his companions said, "Master, the crowds are all around you pressing hard!" Jesus said, "Somebody did touch Me!" ' There are the crowds and the individual—only the setting is changed, the fact not at all. Those about our Lord were conscious only of the crowds; He was aware of the individual.

And He has not changed. The crowds may enclose us 'pressing hard', until one by one we are overwhelmed with a sense of our own insignificance, but in His mercy, He sees and remembers us. When lacking courage, we seek to lose ourselves in the crowd. He judges us and calls us back to truth and life.

That is the wonderful thing about the Gospel of Jesus—it is so relevant. More and more we move in crowds; but at the deepest levels, the crowds break up to reveal us as individuals. And He is there to meet our need.

One of His most gracious acts recorded in the Gospels was His instant recognition of that woman who wished to touch but the hem of His garment; His best-loved set of stories centred in the value of one son, one coin, one sheep; His greatest teaching about God as a Spirit, He gave to one woman beside a well, and not a very good woman at that; the last moments of His life He spent giving a word to one man, a robber; and when the message of His triumph over death broke upon the world, it was couched in language that the world has never forgotten: 'Go and tell His disciples—and Peter', one man overwhelmed with his own sin and insignificance.

The crowd may fascinate us for a time, but it cannot satisfy us. Crowd-religion is not enough. Even in this highly organized age, the soul's relation to Jesus is still individual. It is one thing to feel the crowd swirl hard against one, and against Him, but the time comes—if one's inmost need is to be met—when the *thronging* must give way to *touching*: the crowd must fade into the background until there are only two luminous spirits face to face in the whole universe, Jesus and oneself. One must reach out one's hand of faith, whatever the crowd does, one must respond to Him as an individual, with the whole of one's being. 'Love,' as Hocking says, 'has an individualizing power.'

Whoever we are, wherever we are, as individuals, one by one, we matter to Him. He finds us amid the paralysing sense of our own need. Then in very truth the hymn that we have sung so often becomes a fact of our own experience:

> *We touch Him in life's throng and press,*
> *And we are whole again.*

Well Met

I'VE been a good deal about the world, but to this day I've not climbed Greenland's icy mountains, nor visited India's coral strand. The nearest I've come to realizing that old missionary hymn is lifting up my nose where 'the spicy breezes blow soft o'er Ceylon's isle'! But perhaps it is more important that I have stood by the monument of the young bishop who wrote that hymn; Bishop Heber. It is in St Paul's. A great many monuments are in St Paul's; but there is no other quite like this—the inscription memorializes the young bishop as a man *of intense zeal and toleration*.

I like that meeting of virtues, don't you? All too often, it seems, intense zeal is coupled with in-toleration.

Young Heber, with a brilliant mind, entered Oxford at seventeen, and distinguished himself. After two years travel in Germany and Russia, he ministered in England; then he was made Bishop of Calcutta—one of the most extensive dioceses, comprising all India, Ceylon, and—more surprising still —Australia. Though he died at forty-three, he lived long enough to challenge the world with a combination of 'intense zeal and toleration'.

One of the unforgettable characters in Flora Thompson's *Lark Rise*—the story of her limited village—in contrast to the wide world that Bishop Heber knew, was an old man, a devout Methodist, who when the sound of the Angelus bell was borne on the wind from the Roman Catholic chapel in the neighbouring village, would take off his hat and say: 'In my Father's house are many mansions.'

Toleration is a lovely thing, wherever it is found. The dictionary defines it as 'forbearance, the recognition of right of private judgement in religious matters, liberty to uphold one's religious opinions and forms of worship'.

So many seem to think of it as a negative quality, a kind of easy-going attitude of the person who 'tolerates' anything, because he has no fixed ideas, no loyalties; much less, intense zeal. That, of course, is not toleration—it may be indifference, or laziness. Dr Elton Trueblood sets it out clearly in his *Foundations of Civilization*. 'The present high regard for tolerance,' he says, 'is shown by many clichés which pass for conversation. "Each man has a right to his own view", is one. "A man's religion is his own private business", is another. These seem, superficially, to have a certain validity, but they will not stand up under analysis. . . . When we begin to probe beneath the surface we find that what great numbers of our people mean by freedom of religion is merely a glorified indifference. They think, and some of them say, that they believe in freedom of religion because they believe religion to be unimportant. Great numbers of our people, who are themselves wholly pagan in their lives, pride themselves on being wonderfully tolerant in matters of worship. Their real meaning is: "I can't understand, for the life of me, why anybody wants to do anything so silly as to worship God, who probably does not exist, or to spend a Sunday morning in a stuffy old church when he might be horseback riding or swimming at the beach, but I certainly won't do a thing to stop him. I tell you I'm broadminded in these matters. I don't care whether a man is a Jew or Christian or whatever; I won't stop him; and if I want to be a pagan, I don't want him to stop me." This is the lowest intellectual level on which the contemporary glorification of tolerance appears.'

Such an attitude is far removed from tolerance, as young Bishop Heber understood it, in thought and action, when he matched it with zeal. Tolerance doesn't bloom out of indifference, selfishness, or uncertainty—it's not a limp negative thing, it's a positive thing. Paul set down the core of it in Romans 14. Alive or dead, he says, we are each answerable to God. That is where the easy-going secularist goes astray; he doesn't start by acknowledging that fact. But once this important issue is seen clearly—and we acknowledge the divine sovereignty of God—then a number of other things come straight. For it is soon clear that there are some things incompatible with that which we cannot do. One of them is to exercise the right of sitting in judgement on others.

See how Paul puts it: 'Whether we live, we live unto the Lord; and whether we die, we die unto the Lord; whether we live therefore, or die, we are the Lord's. . . . But why dost thou judge thy brother? or why dost thou set at nought thy brother? for we shall all stand before the judgement seat of Christ. For it is written, As I live, saith the Lord, every knee shall bow to Me, and every tongue confess to God. *So then every one of us shall give an account of himself to God. Let us not therefore judge one another any more; but judge this rather, that no man put a stumbling-block or an occasion to fall in his brother's way.*'

Paul, of course, is referring to two matters that no longer concern us—the observance of special days, and the abstention from certain foods—but the shining core of the matter remains the same. The beginning and ending of life and religion is to glorify God, and the forms which our sincere effort to do that take, must always be of lesser importance. We can't all—even in this day of lively co-operation between members of the world church—confess our faith in the same terms, worship according to the same rites, or even govern our congregations according to the same disciplines. But if we love God with all our hearts and minds and souls, we may do this truly great thing—match intense zeal with tolerance.

Hands

I WONDER if you notice people's hands. I do. They fascinate me. I've just come upon a poem about hands; it speaks of:

> Hands that can hold a horse and plough a furrow,
> And wield an oar, and turn and thrust a foil,
> Hands that can still the wild bird from its trembling
> And coax a blossom from the stoniest soil.
>
> Hands that can make the bated breath go singing
> In exaltation to each several part,
> In these dear mortal hands abide my heaven,
> Surely it is the hands inform the heart.

What lovely hands are remembered in that verse—strong hands, swift hands, sympathetic hands. The very memory of them blesses one. But I feel that there is an error in the last assumption. 'Surely,' says the poet, 'it is the hands inform the heart.' Shouldn't it be the other way round—'it is the heart informs the hands'?

Certainly it was that way with our Lord. Haven't you noticed those significant glimpses in Mark's gospel? He sets down our Lord's relationship with people, as revealed in His hands. There is the leper who comes seeking Him. In the fewest possible words, the action of that moment is captured. 'Jesus,' says Mark, 'moved with compassion, put forth His hand, and touched him' (1⁴¹). There are no blurred outlines; it is His heart that moves His hand.

In a further glimpse, Mark shows Him as He takes the children on His knee. See how he puts it: 'He took them up in

His arms, put His hands upon them, and blessed them' (10^{16}).

The crowds continue unceasing in their claims; but always it is His heart that is moved—then His hands. Even a general statement, overheard, seems full of significance to Mark, and he sets it down: 'Such mighty works are wrought by His hands' (6^2).

And His mighty works are continued to this day—not only to the lepers of our society, and the children, the unclean and the unspoiled; but to one here and another there—to a preacher, and to a modern city man searching for words.

Phillips Brooks said nothing of it, but his people did. And when he died, they engaged a sculptor with mallet and chisel to fashion a memorial. But try as he would, the sculptor could not get his work to come right—five times he took his hammer to it, and five times started again. Then suddenly he saw it all clearly—instead of a figure of Phillips Brooks the great preacher, he set up a block of stone and fashioned a figure of the Christ. Only then did he turn his hand to a likeness of the preacher; and in his sculpture he placed the *hand* of Jesus on the shoulder of Phillips Brooks. Then those who knew and loved him were satisfied, for they said: 'That's how it was—Jesus was always first with Phillips Brooks, and His hand, it seemed, was always on his shoulder.'

In another, and more recent setting, Alan Paton has shown us very tenderly the same wonder—for it has nothing whatever to do with time or place. Paton introduces us to an old Negro preacher living and serving away up in the hills. He and his wife have but one son, and one day he goes off to Johannesburg to see what the city can give him. For a time letters come, and then they cease. And the old couple fear the worst, and the old man sets off to find him. A minister in the great city offers him what help he can. He knows the city, he knows its bright lights and their temptations, and its dark alleys where evils lurk. For a week they set out together to pick up the trail of the lost son, and their hearts are full of foreboding. One morning, suddenly, as he receives yet one more kindness from his new city friend, the old preacher from the hills is strangely moved: 'Oh, but you are wonderfully kind,' he says. At that, the city man can only draw himself up suddenly, and rather blunderingly say a glorious thing, that Mark, if he were writing a modern gospel, would set down in its shining pages: 'I am not kind. I am a selfish and sinful man, but Jesus Christ has placed His hand on me, that is all.'

And who among us, this very hour, can say more—or dare say less?

After Easter

DID you have a good Easter? I wonder how you kept it. Easter is such a high-water mark that we speak of 'before Easter', 'Easter', and 'after Easter'. And now we are come to that period called 'after Easter'. It might be something of a surprise to you, as it was to me, to discover that these actual words are in the New Testament. Prefaced by one other, they make up a very striking text: 'Intending after Easter' (Acts 12⁴).

What Herod had in mind, of course, was the Passover—since he was unfamiliar with the word as we know it. But the translators of our Authorized Version used the word Easter to suggest the time of year, and a parallel feast. So this single instance of the word 'Easter' is something of an anachronism.

From the earliest days of Christianity down to the present, Easter has been celebrated with great joy. In very early times, it was the habit of Christians to salute each other on the morning of the Resurrection day, with 'Christ is risen!' This lovely custom is retained now, as far as I know, only in the Orthodox Church. But we all feel a lifting of the heart on Easter Day.

It is a little difficult to say where the word 'Easter' itself came from. Some think it was derived from *Eostre*, a Saxon deity whose feast was celebrated each spring, about the time of the Christian festival. They say that the name was retained, though the significance of the feast was changed. Others are as sure that we owe the name of our feast of Resurrection to the word *Oster*, meaning rising.

At this date there is no sure means of checking the origin of the name—nor does it greatly matter. We know what we mean by the word 'Easter'. It has become hallowed by a thousand associations. To some it means—on one side of the world, at least—but the breaking of the spring, with its release from the hard disciplines of winter. And how lovely that is, with its new life—the fattening buds on the trees, tiny crocuses springing up, daffodils in the long grass, and hazel catkins hanging frail and golden in the sun. To others Easter means little more than a long week-end, a holiday, the last chance to get away to the beach for bathing or boating before winter sets in. But to many thousands of us, Easter still means all that it meant to Christians of the first century—and more, because we have their experience to add to our own.

'Intending after Easter', the words read. And we are kin with Herod to this extent, at least, that we are people of intentions. Herod's were evil intentions; and he was only waiting for the feast to be at an end, in order to get on with them. He had already disposed of one of the apostles, and only waited a suitable opportunity to take away the life of another. After Easter, he told himself, there would be a suitable opportunity; so he darkly nursed his plans, 'intending after Easter' to put them into operation.

Our intentions are good—especially whilst the Easter hymns and the Easter messages are echoing in our ears. Whatever may have been allowed to mar our year, we are ready to cast off sloth during Lent. And as the great Easter Day approaches, if at no other time, we are found making our way churchwards. There our hearts are solemnized, and we come near to identifying our own sins with those that long ago compassed the death of Jesus. In the solemn service of the Church, we catch again a vision of the milling crowd that clamoured for His death; we trail once again with the curious, the angry, and the faithful out to that Cross, set stark on a hill, beyond the city wall. And because the burden of our share in the world's sin is unbearable in sudden sight of that Cross we cast it down—appropriating as we can the forgiveness that Jesus begged for those who hanged Him there.

So we remember His death—each of us 'intending after Easter' to live in the light of that love that will never let us go. Easter Day—the Day of Resurrection, the day of triumph over death—but quickens those intentions of ours with a new wonder.

After Easter we intend to give the things of our faith a greater place in our lives. We intend, because of what we have seen at Easter, never to write 'failure' over the issues of God—for always there is the third day. We intend to be in no wise identified with Judas the betrayer; to be more loyal in our personal allegiance than Peter—convinced that our hearts are made of sturdier stuff; never for a moment to allow the doubts of Thomas to assail our certainties—we *know* that He is risen! We intend to identify ourselves more closely with Mary, who loved greatly—last at the Cross, and earliest at the Tomb.

We intend 'after Easter', to sit down and read right through the story of that triumph—as set down in John's gospel. We intend to follow it up with an eager, uninterrupted reading of the book of Acts—the whole story at one sitting. We intend, after Easter, to read more books and modern stories of what that same resurrection power is doing in the lives of men and women today. We intend to be more faithful in our attendance on worship—even when visitors call unexpectedly, or the day is sunny enough to be in the garden or out in the car. We intend to make some room for quiet thought in our necessarily busy lives—and more room for prayer. Yes, we *intend* to do all these things—after Easter.

And *now* it is after Easter!

But we had better own up. This is not the first Easter we have kept; this is not the first time we have intended to do all these things after Easter. Easter intentions, like New Year resolutions, alas, are very inclined to weaken as the days go by. I know that, and you know it. I talked one afternoon, in the midst of a busy itinerary, with Muriel Lester of Kingsley Hall. We began by going over some of the remarkable social work that she and her colleagues have been able to do; then we spoke of more personal things—these things, our high intentions and our poor performances. Few, I suppose, know human nature better than Muriel Lester, and she told me with a smile of one old East End woman who had been in grave trouble. At first, when charged with breaking her promises and doing wrong, she vowed innocence. But when further evidence was brought against her, she broke down, and said through her tears: 'Oh, Miss! I'm as good a woman as God ever made . . . only I can't live up to it.'

Now isn't that your trouble, and mine? It certainly sounds like Paul's trouble. It's not that we lack good intentions—we don't—but we lack the strength to carry them out. You remember how Paul put it—in Romans 7^{18-25} (and it is more striking in Moffatt's translation). 'In me,' he says, 'that is in my flesh, no good thing dwells, I know; the wish is there, but not the power of doing what is right. I cannot be good as I want to be, and I do wrong against my wishes. . . . I want to do what is right, but wrong is all I can manage; I cordially agree with God's law, so far as my inner self is concerned, but then I find another law in my members which conflicts with the law of my mind. . . . Miserable wretch that I am! Who will rescue me?' And then he adds, with a note of Resurrection triumph: 'God will! Thanks be to Him, through Jesus Christ our Lord.'

Our intentions—our best Easter intentions—bring us sometimes near to the same kind of despair. But we must go on with Paul, past our anxious query as to who will come to our aid, and say with his assurance, God will! Then what you and I intend after Easter—depending on His almighty strength—can bring us to a new and joyous quality of life.

Lift up your hearts! *Sursum corda!* God can forgive us everything but our unwillingness to put Him to this test.

An Introducer

NEAR us for a time lived a little child—not up to school age—who was very gifted musically. As often as possible my friend gave her help at the piano. And she was about to leave one morning when a small boy arrived. As soon as the little one spied her playmate, she turned to my friend with the earnest plea: 'Don't go yet, please don't go yet: I want to tell Teddy which is him, and which is you'—which charming effort meant, 'I want to introduce Teddy to you.'

Isn't it true that some of the finest things in the world have been done by people with just those intentions? There was that little handful of fishermen beside Galilee. They were well known to each other; but there was a day when one of them came with great news written all over his face: 'I want to introduce you to—well, to One whom I've found!'

The sacred pages where that story is set down are full of things like that. Five thousand people to be fed. But how? Two hundred penny-worth of bread—seven pounds in our money—would not be sufficient for so many. But Andrew has the answer, and he comes forward, in the same character in which we have seen him already—as Introducer. 'There is a lad here with five barley loaves, and two small fishes,' he says, 'but what are they among so many?' Andrew, however, has such wonderful faith in his Master, that he sees some possibility even in that small provision, and with confidence looks down into the face of the lad, and brings him forward.

> *A quick eye had Andrew. He it was amid*
> *The multitudes, that marked the lad,*
> *And what his basket, and how much it had.*

There was another occasion when a handful of Greeks came

seeking his Master. They came first to Philip, attracted perhaps by his Greek name, and begged of him an introduction.
But Philip did not feel sure what to do. The Master was no
lover of curiosity-hunters; He might think it a liberty to in-
trude just then, at Jerusalem's great feast, when every eye was
upon Him. So Philip went to Andrew, and asked his advice.
He knew the Master better than to have any fears; he was sure
He would be glad to see any strangers who came with such
a request, and at once volunteered to introduce them.

It was his old work—that of the Introducer. It was what he
began with, and what I have no doubt he continued with to
the end. And surely no better work can be conceived. Andrew,
it would seem, was no orator—indeed, scarcely a preacher at
all—but he was a friend of Jesus, and an adept at introducing
others to his Friend.

The Greeks came with the query: 'Sir, we would see Jesus!'
And many a time since, men have come with the same question—and they do so still—though not maybe in words, so
clear-cut. But the Kingdom still has need of its Andrews.

Someone has said of one of our own day: 'She introduced
me to Christianity by an inner door, not to its encumbering
forms and doctrines, but to its heart of fire.' That is a lovely
tribute, isn't it? With the same up-to-date realism, Archbishop
Temple said: 'The important fact to remember is that we are
not trying to solve other people's problems and meet their
needs and make them like us. We are trying to introduce them
to One who for them, and for us, can solve problems, meet
needs, and make us like Himself.' That is the heart of the
matter.

You have noticed that Andrew began by bringing Peter to
Jesus. He did not order him. He did not say, 'Go'; he said,
'Come'. I think I see him linking his arm with that of his
brother, as he eagerly utters those words: 'Come and see.' He
did not say, 'Have you found Christ?' but 'I have found Christ'.

One thing is certain: if we would do this task of introduction,
we must have the wisdom and tact and graciousness of Andrew.
It never seems enough to confront one, as at a pistol-point,
with 'Are you saved?' That kind of religion may be some

kind of religion; but it is not, I think, the religion of Andrew, and it lacks the essential winsomeness of the Master of Andrew. 'I once knew a man,' said Dr John Foster, 'who made a practice of asking everyone he met, "Have you found Christ?" When the accounts are entered up,' he adds, speaking of the reception such words received, 'that man will find himself responsible for a considerable stock of blasphemy in the world!' Not so Andrew.

Legend says that later Andrew introduced his Master in Greece, and in Russia, and was at last crucified on an X-shaped cross. In the fourth century of the Christian Church, a Greek monk removed his bones to Scotland—to the coast of Fife, where a church was built. In time a town grew up, known in all the world today as St Andrews. Andrew became Scotland's patron saint, and his cross her national flag. When King James the First came to found a Scottish Order of Knighthood, he called it the Order of St Andrew.

Whatever can be said of legend, this much is true—we should all like to belong to the order of St Andrew. And we may. 'Do you know what I would like to be called?' asked Grayson. 'I cannot imagine,' replied his friend. 'Well, I'd like to be called an introducer.' 'It is a good name,' his friend replied. 'It's a wonderful name,' said Grayson with his face aglow, 'and it's about the biggest and finest work in the world.' It is.

Words and Deeds

I LIKE a good autobiography. There was a good deal in Sir Alfred Munnings's *An Artist's Life* that held little interest for me; but I shall always be grateful to the past-President of the Royal Academy for the word-picture of his old father. He kept a mill at Mendham, and among other delights, he drove a fast grey mare in a dog-cart, and rejoiced in the fellowship of his friends on market-day.

But it was a small action of his at home that pleased me most. Whenever he chanced to see a cart-load of wheat pass his window during family prayers, it was his practice instantly to jump up and run out, to make sure that it was good. Then, content, he would come back and go on with his prayers.

He was a great believer in deeds. He would have rejoiced in old John Lydgate, who set it down plainly several centuries before—in 1400 to be exact: 'Woord is but wynd: leave woord and take the deede.' Moffatt's modern translation of 1 John 3[18] has the same emphasis: 'Let us put our love not into words or into talk, but into deeds, and make it real.' I should like to have met the old miller of Mendham. However beautiful words may be, they are not enough.

This was plainly underlined in the ministry of our Lord. Nor can we forget His story of the Priest and the Levite—they were religious men both of them, but their words did not issue in deeds. The unfortunate wayfarer came from Jerusalem to Jericho, and fell among thieves. The road was notorious enough —surrounded by desert, scored by *wadis*, rocky water-courses, dry except in the very rainy season. There was no lack of excellent hiding-places.

How long the poor fellow lay on the roadside, robbed, and beaten insensible, nobody knows. We only know that as he lay there a Priest came by, then a Levite—each on his way from religious duties in the Temple. And each passed by on the other side. No doubt each had his reasons, or excuses. Who could know whether the robbers who had attacked the poor wretch were not at that moment waiting for another victim? In any case, the fellow looked beyond casual help— he might even be dead. And that would mean that if either stayed to move him, he would be disqualified from performing his religious duties in the Temple. A recent speaker has suggested a little cynically that perhaps the Priest and the Levite were hurrying down to Jericho to attend a meeting of the Distressed Travellers' Aid Society.

In contrast to these men of fine words, Jesus told of the man of deeds—the Good Samaritan. Interpret the story as you choose, excuse the Priest and the Levite as you may, the contrast is unmistakenly clear. Jesus was not underrating the worth of words, or the service of God in His place of worship—far from it. He was a regular worshipper all His days, and some of the well-loved words of the Old Testament and the House of God were on His lips to the end. But Jesus expected words to issue in deeds.

It was no trivial thing that the Samaritan did—pouring in oil as he bent over the poor fellow, and binding up his wounds. He ran the risks that the others had avoided in lingering in the place. More than that, he was hindered in his own affairs, as he set him upon his own beast, and supporting him, got him to the inn. And before he left, he had a word with the inn-keeper—and dug into his own pocket, saying: 'Take care of him; and whatsoever thou spendest more, I, when I come back again, will repay thee.'

Christ's emphasis here—as in so many of His stories—is on the 'how much more'. If an outsider, a Samaritan, a man of no fine words, can do such a shining deed for a poor wretch with no special claims upon him, *how much more* should be forthcoming from a man of faith?

And we still have to find the answer to that question in modern terms.

Acknowledgements

MY thanks are due to the following Authors and Publishers for permission to quote from copyright works:

The Author and Latimer House Ltd, an extract from *Bristol Fashion* by Hugh Redwood; the Authors and Jonathan Cape Ltd, extracts from *Mary Webb: Her Life and Work* by Thomas Moult, *Cornish Years* by Anne Treneer, and *Collected Poems* by Teresa Hooley; Hamish Hamilton Ltd, and the Editor, Edward R. Murrow, extracts from contributions by Sir Miles Thomas and V. Sackville-West to *This I Believe*; the Author and Hodder & Stoughton Ltd, extract from *The Man Who Made Wine* by J. M. Scott; the Author and George Allen & Unwin Ltd, extract from *Memoirs of Childhood and Youth* by Albert Schweitzer; the Author and Faber & Faber Ltd, extract from *I Lived in a Suitcase* by Margaret Mackay; S.C.M. Press Ltd, extract from *The Significance of Jesus* by W. R. Maltby; the Author and Methuen & Co. Ltd, extract from *Govan Calling* by George MacLeod; the Author and James Nisbet & Co. Ltd, extract from *Servant of the Word* by H. H. Farmer; the Author and Eyre & Spottiswoode Ltd, extract from *Foundations of Civilization* by Elton Trueblood.

R. F. S.